Gateway

GATEWAY

A Visitor's Companion

John T. Tanacredi, Ph.D.

with Curtis J. Badger

STACKPOLE
BOOKS

Published by
STACKPOLE BOOKS
5067 Ritter Road
Mechanicsburg, PA 17055
www.stackpolebooks.com

Printed in the United States of America

Cover Design by Mark Olszewski
Cover photograph and color-section photographs by Don Riepe

Photograph credits:
P. A. Buckley, 121
Robert Cook, 22, 81, 85
Thomas H. Davis, 27
National Park Service, 19, 20, 24
Don Riepe, 12, 16, 17, 25, 27, 29, 32, 39, 47, 48, 53, 58, 64, 66, 67, 72, 76, 77, 87, 88, 93, 94, 101, 108, 110, 112, 119, 124, 126, 135
John Tanacredi, 7, 9, 34
U.S. Fish and Wildlife Service, 11
Brooks Vaughn, 5

First Edition

10 9 8 7 6 5 4 3 2

Library of Congress Cataloging-in-Publication Data

Tanacredi, John T.
    Gateway ; a visitor's companion / John T. Tanacredi, with Curtis
J. Badger. — 1st ed.
        p. cm.
    Includes index.
    ISBN 0-8117-2546-4
    1. Gateway National Recreation Area (N.J. and N.Y.)—
Guidebooks. I. Badger, Curtis J. II. Title.
F128.65.G38T36   1995
917. 49'46—dc20   95-21523
                                                          CIP

To Julianne, Jeannine, and Ryan

CONTENTS

Acknowledgments

Gateway is the result of hundreds of dedicated National Park Service employees who over the years, along with a host of other people, have had a keen interest in and concern for our National Park system. Without their contributions since the park's inception in 1972, this book would not be possible.

There are those, however, who stand out in their contributions to this book's completion. First and foremost, I want to thank Sam Holmes for bringing me into the National Park Service more than eighteen years ago and for his tutelage, which continues to inspire me. His first review of this project put me on the right track to completion. To a dear friend and mentor, P. A. Buckley, go my deepest gratitude and fondest appreciation for his guidance, as well as for his insights and his role as an impassioned Gateway advocate.

My deep appreciation goes to those who were instrumental in developing the material on species and who provided extensive input to specialized sections: Robert P. Cook (mammals, reptiles and amphibians); Donald Riepe (invertebrates, butterflies and moths); E. Ann Scaglione and Dave Taft (fisheries); Michael D. Byer, Richard Salter, and Bonnie Zarrillo (plants); Tom Hoffman, Michael Thomas, Peter Bathurst, and Michael Adlerstein (historical aspects); Francine Buckley and P. A. Buckley (birds); and Ellen Falvo (literature corroboration and initial species list compilation).

A special thanks goes to those who took their time to review the early drafts of this manuscript: Bob McIntosh (whom I would care to thank specially for his guidance as General Superintendent at Gateway for nine years and who allowed me a special gift during his tenure—to grow as a researcher, scientist, and professional), Hooper Brooks, Tom Fox, Jeanette Parker, Bruce Lane, Dave Avrin, Bob Cunningham, Dave Taft, and Art

Stewart. To Kevin C. Buckley, presently the General Superintendent at
Gateway, a very special thank you for giving me the time and opportunity and for having the foresight that allowed me to put this work
together. Brian Feeney, Bob Cook, Mike Byer, Don Riepe, Brooks Vaughn
and P. A. Buckley provided photos. Dave Taft's artwork is a wonder to
behold; my attempts at capturing the nature of this park on paper pale in
comparison to his sketches.

Special thanks goes to Laura A. Barba and Jennifer Smith, who toiled
to retype and organize the initial manuscript, and to the following
National Park Service people, who have all contributed to Gateway's
natural resource program over the years: Jim Allen, Joe Antosca, Herb
Cables, Rich Clark, Skip Cole, Mary Foley, John Guthrie, Larry May, Ken
Morgan, Herb Olsen, Jose Rosario, Mary Rust, Mary Gibson-Scott,
Manny Strampf, Bill Shields, and Mike Soukup.

Curtis Badger's uncanny observational and editorial ability provided
a rewrite of this manuscript, giving it all of its noteworthiness. Errors
of omission or accuracy, though, are mine alone. Sally Atwater, Anne
Schreiber, and Val Gittings of Stackpole Books were most important in
guiding me through the editorial process, and to them goes a warm heart-
felt thanks.

INTRODUCTION

Gateway National Recreation Area is one of more than 360 parks that make up America's National Park System. It was the culmination of early 1960s influences, including a Bureau of Outdoor Recreation report on urban recreational needs, and the foresight of Newark's Mayor Kenneth Gibson and New York City's Mayor John V. Lindsay. Formally established by the U.S. Congress on October 27, 1972, Gateway and Golden Gate Park in San Francisco became the first urban national recreation areas within the National Park System.

Since Gateway's inception its mission has been to bring the National Park Service message of preservation and protection to the few remaining open spaces in New York City while fostering the natural, cultural, and recreational resources of one of the most complex and populous areas of the world. Advocates for such a National Park entity, such as the late Congressman William Fitz Ryan, a New York City public advocate, the late Shelden Pollack, and Stanley Tankel, helped spearhead Congress's request to incorporate abandoned or obsolete military facilities in New Jersey and New York.

The diversity of Gateway reflects the diversity of the urban area it serves. The park includes fascinating natural resources, such as wild beaches and salt marshes that are home to endangered species of animals and plants. Park visitors will also find a historic airfield, forts dating from the 1800s, the nation's oldest operating lighthouse, sports complexes, environmental education facilities, community gardens, and a flight center for model airplanes.

Unique to Gateway is its location, a place where the open Atlantic meets the land, where the salt waters of the ocean mix with the brackish waters of bays and fresh waters of rivers and streams. This estuarine ecosystem is rich and complex, a place both fragile and resilient.

Twenty-five million people live in and around New York City, making it one of the greatest metropolitan areas of the world. And yet Gateway's estuary system—this rendezvous of the Atlantic Ocean, the Hudson and Raritan Rivers, and Long Island Sound—continues to function much as it did before there was even a village settlement.

This *Visitor's Companion* is a general guide to Gateway—to its natural system of beaches and marshes and bays, as well as to its history, culture, and the humans who have lived in this place over the centuries. It is not a comprehensive field guide, nor can its scope include all that is within the boundaries of the park.

Instead, this *Companion* is intended to give you a feel for Gateway's character, to spark your interest, to make you curious, and to encourage you to learn more. Gateway is a complex place, a diverse assemblage of nature, history, buildings, and people. The *Visitor's Companion* will start you on an enjoyable journey of discovery in this fascinating urban national park.

When to Visit Gateway National Recreation Area

The New York City region enjoys a northeast, Atlantic coastal climate. Winter temperatures range from 20°F to 40°F and summer temperatures, from 70°F to 90°F. Open 365 days a year, Gateway is a year-round park that offers indoor and outdoor activities for any season. Birders are afield throughout the year at Jamaica Bay Wildlife Refuge and at Sandy Hook. During spring and summer, the primary tourist seasons, there are abundant opportunities for both wildlife observation and beach use.

For a brochure of seasonal events, write to General Superintendent, c/o Public Affairs Office, Gateway National Recreation Area, Headquarters Building, Floyd Bennett Field, Brooklyn, NY 11234. If you would like to receive future announcements, request that your name and address be placed on the Gateway mailing list.

GATEWAY TO THE SEA

On the beach at Breezy Point an endangered piping plover nests amid a scattering of shells just beyond the reach of high tide. The plover shares the beach with hundreds of other birds. Least and common terns build shallow nests in the sand and lay clutches of speckled eggs. Sanderlings and red knots forage along the water's edge, probing the sand for tiny invertebrates. Although the terns and plovers are nesting, red knots and sanderlings are just passing through, pausing to refuel before resuming their migration to nesting areas of their own farther north.

Watch the coming and going of the beach birds, listen as the noisy conversation of terns fills the air, and you begin to realize what a remarkably prolific natural system this is. And in the case of Breezy Point, a sandy peninsula that separates the Atlantic Ocean and Rockaway Inlet east of New York City, the scene is even more remarkable.

Forget the terns and plovers for a moment and from Breezy Point look to the north. What you see is the Manhattan skyline, punctuated by the twin towers of the World Trade Center and the spire of the Empire State Building. In the foreground, a little to your left, is Brooklyn, and the huge Ferris wheel you see across the inlet is a Coney Island landmark. Look to the east and you will see planes taking off and landing. That would be John F. Kennedy International Airport, one of the busiest in the world. The Concorde you see gaining altitude will be in London in a little over three hours.

Surely this is one of the most incredible juxtapositions in nature. You can stand amid a setting that is thoroughly wild and timeless, where the human hand has touched only lightly, yet just beyond is one of the busiest centers of commerce in the world.

It is, unarguably, a testimony to the resilience of nature, yet it also is a confirmation of the human need to include in our lives an untrodden

Gateway's position along the Atlantic flyway of bird migration provides the visitor with an opportunity to observe approximately one-third of the bird species in North America.

portion of earth where the birds and animals and fish and insects carry on as they always have, and always will. It took a great deal of foresight and determination to save Breezy Point and places like it, but today we realize that these open spaces are as necessary to the lives of the people of the New York area as are the skyscrapers, offices, freeways, and airports.

Cities fuel the human need to work and communicate; wild places like Breezy Point are essential to the human spirit.

Breezy Point is part of the Gateway National Recreation Area, comprising several sites in the Hudson-Raritan estuary, where the fresh waters of inland rivers meet the sea. Two sandy peninsulas frame the entrance to the estuary—Breezy Point in New York and Sandy Hook in New Jersey—forming a natural gateway through which millions of immigrants have passed as they sought a new life in a new world.

And thus when Congress created the urban park in 1972, the name Gateway seemed especially appropriate. The sandy peninsulas form a literal gateway to New York Harbor, but in a metaphorical sense, they represent a gateway to new lives, to renewed hope. Today the metaphor continues, though slightly changed. For contemporary visitors, many of whom are city dwellers, Gateway is an entry both to learning about our rapidly changing environment and to enjoying a uniquely beautiful setting.

Gateway NRA contains more than 26,000 acres, bringing together sites as diverse as historic forts and wildlife sanctuaries. There are three major sites, or units, in the park, and each has its own character and amenities. Included are ocean beaches such as Breezy Point on the Rockaway Peninsula, Jamaica Bay Wildlife Refuge, Floyd Bennett Field in Brooklyn, Staten Island on the opposite shore of the estuary, and the Sandy Hook peninsula on the northern New Jersey coast.

Gateway is perhaps America's most eclectic national park. It includes a historic airport, Floyd Bennett Field, where Wiley Post, Amelia Earhart, Howard Hughes, and John Glenn once flew. Until it was replaced by La Guardia Airport, Floyd Bennett Field was New York City's international airport. There are also a nineteenth-century fort, a lighthouse, a former lifesaving station, and a rare maritime forest on Sandy Hook; a seaplane base on Staten Island; defunct Nike missile launch sites at Fort Tilden and Sandy Hook; a wildlife refuge with more than 325 species of birds; and ocean beaches still sufficiently wild that terns and plovers can call them home.

Gateway thus brings together a collection of sites that in former incarnations have played a variety of roles, from national defense, travel, and commerce to recreation and wildlife sanctuary.

The various elements of Gateway began to gain protection as the city grew and its citizens and leaders became aware of the need to protect some of the unique natural areas. Jamaica Bay Wildlife Refuge, a sanctuary of some 9,000 acres, was created by New York City in 1953. At Sandy Hook, the New Jersey State Park Commission in the 1960s took action to preserve the rare maritime holly forest on the western side of the peninsula. In New York, citizen groups from the Rockaway Peninsula successfully fought the building of a highrise complex and thus preserved the natural quality of a stretch of ocean beach.

These various sites came under the umbrella of Gateway NRA when the park was created by Congress in 1972. Gateway has grown over the years through the inclusion of other unique historic and natural sites, and it has improved these places by building relationships with city, state, federal, and private partners. Stricter standards established in the 1970s

Urban development was halted on Breezy Point in the early 1980s. The destruction of unfinished buildings cleared the land for restoration of the natural landscape and expansion of Gateway.

have reduced air pollution, and waterways have been cleaned by improved sewage treatment systems. A growing awareness of the natural beauty of beaches and wetlands has prompted community clean-up efforts.

The result is a remarkably diverse park, where visitors are offered activities ranging from nature study and fishing to model airplane flying and gardening. In the chapters that follow, we will take a close-up look at this urban sanctuary and its various components and constituents.

EBB AND FLOW

Imagine for a moment that there were no such thing as New York City. After all, when measured in geologic time, the buildings and freeways are recent additions, a wink of an eye in the long-range process of species evolution and geologic history.

Go back four centuries and you will find Algonquin villages scattered along the banks of what we now call Jamaica Bay and Lower New York Bay. The shallow waters were rich in marine life, as the shell middens we find today attest. There were expansive salt marshes, broad beaches, and plentiful fish. Striped bass would enter the estuary in early spring and swim up the Tappan Sea to the Hudson River. There they would spawn, raising another generation of marine migrants that would trade between the salt waters of the coastal bays and ocean and the fresh waters of inland rivers.

Go back even further than the Algonquins and you will find a land vastly different from what we know today. Fifteen thousand years ago Pleistocene glaciers extended across Canada and southward through the northern United States roughly to the south shore of Long Island and New Jersey. Because a great deal of the planet's water was locked in glacial ice, the sea level was much lower—more than 350 feet below present-day sea level. At the end of the Pleistocene ice ages, just before the glaciers melted in retreat, the New York City shoreline was approximately 100 miles east of where it is today. What we now know as New York Harbor would have been many miles from the open sea.

If you could look back 550 million years ago, Long Island would appear as a tiny fraction of an island arc that once extended from Newfoundland to Alabama. Later, Long Island's volcanic bedrock collided with the land mass that would become the North American continent.

Coastal spartina marshes fringe the park.

This collision pushed up the continental edge, subjecting the exposed rock to erosion and causing the extreme edge of the continental crust to sink beneath the sea. Sediment erosion that has continued since then has formed our familiar East Coast beaches.

The grinding of the glaciers had a profound effect on the geology of the Gateway ecosystem, laying bare bedrock tens of kilometers thick. Although the glaciers have been gone for thousands of years, their influence is readily seen in the striations in bare bedrock in the Bronx, and in the glacial erratics in Prospect Park in Brooklyn. Fly over Manhattan on a clear day and you can see how glacially sculpted bedrock helped form the city skyline. The huge buildings follow the undulating profile of outcrops of thick bedrock, which forms a natural building foundation.

When the glaciers began melting and the sea level rose, barrier beaches, lagoons, and salt marshes were formed. Sediments that had been scraped from massive bedrock and trapped in glacial ice were freed and were swept to the coast by rivers and streams, helping to form the beaches we enjoy today at Sandy Hook and Breezy Point. Pick up a handful of sand and examine it with a magnifying glass. You will see the remains of ancient mountains—fragments of quartz, garnet, and magnetite—washed down from the highlands to the coast and mixed with the calcium bits of seashells.

Consider the geologic history of the Gateway region, and you realize that the system is dynamic on several levels. On a daily basis the tides rise and fall, carrying with them sand and sediment. Storm surf crashes onto the beach at an oblique angle, creating a littoral drift that sends sand from one area of the beach to another. A northeaster broaches the island, creating an overwash fan and sending salt water into brackish lagoons behind the beach.

On a long-term basis, the sea level rises and falls. Glaciers retreat and advance. On the coastal plain, even small changes have major implications. Since 1900 the sea level has risen about a foot. As a result, our great-grandfathers' potato and corn fields are now salt marshes; their salt marshes are now bay bottom.

Like birds and animals, a coastal ecosystem survives by adaptation. The beaches at Sandy Hook and the Rockaway Peninsula are flat and broad, so when a storm hits, its energy is dissipated over a wide area. Winter northeasters can actually cover parts of an island. For developed beaches, such events can be disastrous, but on natural beaches overwashes are common and advantageous. Flattened overwash fans, usually covered by shell litter, will be prime nesting sites for piping plovers, terns, and black skimmers in the spring.

The wide, low-slung beaches act as a geological shock absorber for the mainland and the shallow bays and salt marshes that are part of the estuary. The beaches are forever changing, sculpted by wind and water, adapting like an amoeba to forces outside the organism. Given the kinetic energy of the ocean and the inertia of land, adaptation is a matter of survival. On the beach, change is the only constant.

The salt marshes protected by the beaches are among the most productive systems in nature. The islands and shorelines of Jamaica Bay—protected by the long arm of Rockaway Peninsula—serve as a vast nursery for myriad marine species. Hardshell clams burrow beneath the bottom, sucking nutrients from the rich water. Mud snails forage on an exposed flat. Periwinkles climb stalks of cordgrass and scrape away nutrients left by high tide. The shallow bay allows sunlight to penetrate its depth, and a variety of grasses cover the bottom. There, small crabs hide from predators, and killifish and mummichogs avoid the search of summer flounder.

Jamaica Bay is the largest contiguous natural portion of the New York Harbor estuary.

Jamaica Bay, like most shallow coastal bays, is a giant protein factory, a machine that begins with the energy of sunlight, converts it to food by photosynthesis, and distributes the sun's energy to an amazing assortment of wild things.

Plants and Animals of the Estuary

In the salt marshes of Jamaica Bay, the primary plant is *Spartina alterniflora*, or salt marsh cordgrass. It is a unique plant for a number of reasons. For one thing, it thrives in a saltwater environment that would bring quick and certain death to most plants. But *Spartina* has adapted to salt water in a wonderful way, using a special membrane to filter out harmful salts while allowing beneficial ones to pass through. *Spartina* thrives in the salt water of the estuary, growing tallest and thickest along the edges of marsh where its roots are immersed twice daily, its stems washed by the flowing tides. It is a remarkable plant, irrigated by pure seawater, engineered to withstand violent coastal storms, a processor and distributor of the solar energy upon which the entire estuary depends.

On the salt marsh, *Spartina alterniflora* is ubiquitous. Along the edges of creeks and bays, it grows in thick stands sometimes to heights of six feet. On the upper marsh, where tidal flow is limited, the grass is shorter, from about six inches to two or three feet, and it grows less dense, often with colonies of *Salicornia*, a tubular, succulent plant that turns brilliant red in the fall.

In the upper elevations, where the salt marsh joins fastland, *Spartina alterniflora* gives way to *Spartina patens*, a shorter, finer grass called salt meadow hay, and *Distichlis spicata*, or salt grass.

The plants define the topography of the estuary, and they change as the salinity of the water gradually drops as the tidal ocean water mixes with the fresh water of rivers and streams. It is a precarious landscape, where only a few inches in elevation separate *Spartina alterniflora* from its smaller, finer cousin, *Spartina patens*, a plant of the higher marsh where tides reach only during the highest periods of the monthly cycles. Each plant has its niche, well defined and precise: *Spartina alterniflora* on the lowest marshes; followed by *S. patens*; *Salicornia*; *Distichlis spicata*, similar in appearance to *S. patens*; sea lavender, with its tiny blue summer flow-

Salt meadow hay, common at higher elevations in the marshes, is finer than salt marsh grass, which is found in lower elevations just at the water's edge.

ers; sea oxeye, a striking, succulent plant with yellow flowers in summer and brown prickly seedheads in winter; marsh elder; groundsel; and, on the lowest fastland, bayberry and holly.

As the salinity of the water gradually drops, the number of wetlands plants increases. The *Spartinas* are joined, and eventually supplanted, by black rush, salt marsh aster, sea pink, loosestrife, threesquare, bulrush, fleabane, and mallow. Dense stands of *Phragmites* can be found in the upper salt marsh and in brackish areas.

This range of plant species may occur over a change in elevation of only one foot or so, and subtle changes in sea level bring about dramatic differences in plant communities. Plant succession can occur quickly as salinity increases or decreases.

The *Spartinas*, however, are the dominant energy converters of the salt marsh. The entire community of marshes, bays, islands, fish, shellfish, birds, and animals begins with these grasses, which collect the energy of the sun in photosynthesis and later distribute it to myriad creatures as the grasses die and are broken down by bacteria. The mixture of bacteria, epiphytic algae, and the cellulose particles of digested *Spartina* form the broad base of the salt marsh food chain, a nutrient-rich soup called detritus.

It is a remarkable but very economical process perfected over millennia of natural selection. Nothing is superfluous. Nothing is left to waste. The system is fragile but perfectly balanced. The plants grow prodigiously during the summer, fed by nutrients swept in with the tides, storing the energy of the sun during the long, unshaded days. Then in the fall this stored energy is released as the exposed stems and leaves die. The plant collapses to the marsh floor, and the bacteria attack. The single-cell bacteria are so small they cannot consume bits of *Spartina* in the traditional manner. Instead, the plant is digested outside the cells of the animals, and as a result, the *Spartina* is reduced to progressively smaller bits and pieces.

This rich detritus mixture—bacteria, plant remains, larvae, free-flowing eggs, and algae stirred by tidal action into a nutritious broth—is eaten by protozoans that live in the shallow water, by the filter-feeding burrowing worms of the tidal flats, by oysters, clams, mussels, nematodes, snails, insect larvae, fiddler crabs, and such small fish as menhaden and silversides, which either filter the nutrients from the water or eat them with bottom mud.

The detritus eaters are preyed upon by animals higher on the food chain: larger fish, blue crabs, waterfowl, wading birds, and raccoons and other mammals. A clapper rail stalks the cordgrass marsh, spearing an unsuspecting periwinkle snail from a grass stem. A great blue heron waits patiently in a shallow stream, then surprises a passing killifish. An osprey circles over the open bay, dives, and comes up with a fish in its talons. A fisherman drifts in a small boat along Rockaway Inlet, hoping to entice a flounder with an offering of squid and minnows.

Coastal salt marshes, such as those found in lower New York Harbor, were once considered wasteland, home of dangerous snakes and disease-carrying insects. In good American entrepreneurial fashion, marshes were drained and filled and converted to farmland, residential communities, industrial sites, and airports. We are finally coming to the realization, though, that salt marshes play a vital role in nature and in human society. They protect against storms, filter our water supply, and serve as a prolific nursery for fish, shellfish, birds, and animals.

The marshes of Jamaica Bay provide ample evidence of the fecundity of this unique coastal environment. Jamaica Bay Wildlife Refuge is considered a crown jewel of Gateway, and it takes only a brief visit to understand why.

Jamaica Bay

The Jamaica Bay–Breezy Point unit of Gateway is the largest and most diverse section of the park. There you find the 10,000-acre Jamaica Bay Wildlife Refuge, Floyd Bennett Field, Plumb Beach, and a number of sites on the Rockaway Peninsula, such as Jacob Riis Park, Fort Tilden, and Breezy Point. Activities range from environmental education programs to sunbathing. Amenities include a marina, a horseback riding stable, and a restaurant concession on Canarsie Pier overlooking the bay. The pier is accessible by boat, and there is ample parking for the variety of year-round events.

Jamaica Bay Wildlife Refuge

Jamaica Bay is located in the boroughs of Brooklyn and Queens, with the Shore Parkway (known locally as the Belt Parkway) forming the northern boundary; Rockaway Peninsula the southern boundary; John F. Kennedy International Airport the eastern boundary; and Plumb Beach and Floyd Bennett Field the western boundary.

In a metropolitan area of twenty-five million people, the Jamaica Bay refuge provides a sanctuary for both wildlife and humans. The shallow bay, with its tidal marshes and inlets, sandy beaches, and small islands, is a remarkably productive salt marsh ecosystem with many components.

The bay is fed by the tidal waters of Rockaway Inlet, which connects the protected bay with the open Atlantic. The great natural attraction of Jamaica Bay is the series of islands that covers much of it. These salt marsh islands, covered mainly by *Spartina alterniflora*, form the basis of the Jamaica Bay food chain, supporting life ranging from microscopic phytoplankton and zooplankton to fish, birds, and humans.

The uninhabited islands are home or stopover sites to more than 325 species of birds. Ospreys nest on raised platforms made specifically for

Ospreys were on the brink of extinction until the ban on DDT and other pesticides allowed for their current resurgence. Also called fish hawk, the osprey soars over water, then dives for its prey.

them. Laughing gulls, great black-backed gulls, oystercatchers, and clapper rails build their nests in the marshes, while herons, egrets, and glossy ibis nest in rookeries built in shrubby growth on the higher elevations. Terns, plovers, skimmers, and a variety of shorebirds use the sandy beaches. The dense bayberry thickets provide food and protection from predators for warblers, tanagers, thrushes, and other songbirds as they migrate along the Atlantic Flyway from their winter homes in the tropics to nesting areas in North America.

Jamaica Bay was essentially an undisturbed wilderness until the late 1800s, ranking with Great South Bay and Chesapeake Bay in the production of oysters, finfish, and other seafood. In 1878 the Secretary of War sought to "improve" the bay as a commercial seaport, a proposal that later was backed by the City of New York. Channels 1,000 to 1,500 feet wide were dredged, and the dredge spoil was used to fill marshes and create fastlands where docks and piers could be built.

Later, additional dredging built up salt marsh sites to create Floyd

Bennett Field and John F. Kennedy International Airport (until around 1963 called Idlewild). Still other wetland sites were filled through the disposal of solid waste and sewage sludge. By the time the importance of wetlands was recognized in the late 1960s, nearly half of the original salt marshes of Jamaica Bay had been destroyed. After almost a century of "improvements," the bay's area had been reduced from 25,000 acres to 13,000—a loss of 12,000 acres of pristine tidal salt marsh.

Efforts to protect the bay began in 1938, under the leadership of Mayor Fiorello La Guardia and Parks Commissioner Robert Moses. Moses issued a booklet, "The Future of Jamaica Bay," advocating use of the bay as a public recreation resource. Moses recommended that the city protect the "scenery and waters, preserve wildlife, reduce pollution, and encourage swimming, fishing, and boating." In 1948 the lands of the bay were for-

During peak migration periods, many species of shorebirds crowd the beaches and mudflats.

mally transferred to the New York City Department of Parks to develop according to Moses' long-term plan.

In 1951 Jamaica Bay was surveyed by the U.S. Fish and Wildlife Service to assess its potential as a national wildlife refuge and recreational resource. A report, written by Clarence Cottam, recommended the creation of fresh or brackish impoundments and various food and habitat plantings. The U.S. Fish and Wildlife Service, aided, ironically, by funds from the sale of Migratory Bird Hunting Stamps, was building refuges along the Atlantic coast to provide food and sanctuary for migratory waterfowl.

The impoundments were built in 1953 on a large island near where the visitor center is now located. The project came about through a partnership between the New York City Parks Commission and the New York Transit Authority. The transit authority needed sand to create an embankment along the Rockaway subway line (part of an old Long Island Railroad right-of-way), and in exchange for permission to dredge the material from Jamaica Bay, the transit authority agreed to build dikes to create two freshwater impoundments, the east and west ponds.

After the ponds were constructed, amateur horticulturist Herbert S. Johnson was appointed refuge manager, and he set out to implement the wildlife management programs recommended by Clarence Cottam. Under Johnson's capable and dedicated management, a great variety of native trees and shrubs were planted, many of which Johnson propagated in his own backyard. Habitat enhancement continues today with native plants being propagated in the park's greenhouse at Floyd Bennett Field, and then replanted to restore habitat throughout the park.

Under Johnson's leadership the Jamaica Bay Wildlife Refuge became one of the most important migratory bird sanctuaries in the northeastern United States. In 1972 Congress enacted Public Law 92-592, establishing the Gateway National Recreation Area. Included in the law is the directive that the Secretary of the Interior "shall administer and protect the islands and waters within the Jamaica Bay Unit with the primary aim of conserving the natural resources, fish, and wildlife located therein and shall permit no development or use of this area which is incompatible with this purpose."

Today, the management emphasis at Jamaica Bay continues to be wildlife protection, and most active recreational uses are channeled toward more suitable, less vulnerable sites. Sensitive areas, such as nesting

Herbert Johnson, refuge manager of the park in the 1960s, implemented the program to create the Jamaica Bay Wildlife Refuge.

habitat on island salt marshes, are zoned either "Protection," indicating that access is restricted to protect wildlife, or "Use-by-reservation," meaning an area is closed to the general public except for research, field trips, or other closely monitored educational activities organized by the National Park Service.

The public is welcome 365 days a year to the Jamaica Bay Wildlife Refuge Visitor Center, linked to the mainland by Cross Bay Boulevard at Exit 17 on the Belt. The visitor center, open daily from 8:30 A.M. to 5 P.M., offers interpretive displays, hiking trails, a video, and regularly scheduled programs by park naturalists. Some 80,000 people visit the center each year, with peak visitation during the spring and fall bird migration seasons.

In fall and early winter, the impoundments are filled with Canada geese, mallards, black ducks, northern pintails, gadwalls, and many other species of waterfowl. Shorebirds forage in the shallow water and along the tidal flats that surround the island. In the deeper waters offshore, double-crested cormorants, mergansers, buffleheads, and other diving ducks can be seen.

During spring and fall migrations, the bayberry thickets and other

Nike missile bases built on Rockaway Peninsula during the Cold War have been vacated by the military; they now remain as a landmark.

forested areas of the refuge are filled with flycatchers, warblers, tanagers, orioles, and other neotropical migrants on their way between summer homes in North America and wintering grounds in Central and South America.

The appeal of the Jamaica Bay Wildlife Refuge to birders is not only the great variety of species that may be seen, but also the exceptional diversity of habitats within a fairly limited area. On a leisurely birding hike of perhaps two hours, visitors can explore the salt marsh, tidal flats, open water, freshwater impoundments, grasslands, and forested upland. At any time of year, there will be interesting birds to see and record on your "life list."

The Rockaway Peninsula

The Rockaway Peninsula is a slim finger of land on the southwest tip of Long Island. Several sites on the peninsula are included in Gateway National Recreation Area. Jacob Riis Park, named for the crusading New York journalist, is one of the prime ocean beaches of the region. Swimming and surf fishing are popular here, and there are facilities for softball, baseball, football, and other recreational sports.

Adjacent to Jacob Riis Park is Fort Tilden, a point of defense for New York City intermittently since the War of 1812. Its military presence has in recent years been replaced by a constituency more attuned to recreation and natural history. The Nike missile bunkers are still visible, as are the few sixteen-inch gun emplacements, but the groups you see marching across the meadows and beaches adjacent to these high ground bunkers will be schoolchildren learning about the flora and fauna of a coastal ecosystem, or wildlife biologists banding migratory raptors (the number of hawks and eagles banded during one season exceeded 1,200).

Farthest west, at the peninsula's tip, is Breezy Point, a protected ocean beach where endangered piping plovers, roseate terns, least terns, common terns, black skimmers, and American oystercatchers nest from May until August. In addition, the beach is used by a variety of shorebirds as they migrate in spring and fall. Gulls, principally herring gulls and great black-backed gulls, forage along the shoreline. The thickets behind the primary dunes are home to songbirds and numerous cottontail rabbits.

Park naturalists have reintroduced several species that had been extirpated from this metropolitan region. Eastern hognose snake has been successfully transplanted, as has its chief prey, Fowler's toad. By

The hognose snake has been restored at Gateway through the cooperation of the Bronx Zoological Park; hatchlings are reared there and then released throughout Gateway.

implanting a tiny microchip in the body of each snake, researchers can trace their movements and gauge how well they are being reacclimated.

Breezy Point, while surrounded by the expected trappings of a large city, provides a glimpse of what a wilderness beach was like during the days of the Algonquins. Dolphins and pilot whales have been observed cruising beyond the breakers offshore, and the plovers and terns return each spring to build their nests amid the shell litter. The only difference is that today the birds' chief predator is not the raccoon or ghost crab, but the household cat.

FLOYD BENNETT FIELD

Floyd Bennett Field is in a literal sense a product of the Jamaica Bay ecosystem. A former salt marsh, the airfield was created by the dumping of dredge spoil taken from the bay. In its day, Floyd Bennett Field was the heartbeat of American aviation. When it opened in 1931, it boasted the longest concrete runway in the world. It served the growing aviation industry, and it was the focal point of heroic flights (and not-so-heroic flights—"Wrong-way" Corrigan flew out of Floyd Bennett Field) that captured the imagination of the public.

Wiley Post flew from Floyd Bennett Field in 1933 when he completed a trip around the world in seven days and eighteen hours. Five years later Howard Hughes erased Post's record, circling the globe in three days and nineteen hours. When he landed at Floyd Bennett Field and taxied to a stop on the apron in front of the administration building, 30,000 ecstatic fans welcomed him. The police were called in to control the crowd.

Floyd Bennett Field not only served its share of aviation pioneers, it was named for one. Floyd Bennett, a native of Warrensburg, New York, was one of the first to fly over the North Pole, accompanying explorer Richard E. Byrd on several expeditions. He died at age thirty-eight in 1928 after coming down with pneumonia on a rescue flight. These flights over the pole were considered worthy of our nation's highest military honors, and Floyd Bennett received the Congressional Medal of Honor.

Floyd Bennett Field was decommissioned as a U.S. Navy airfield in 1970 and became part of Gateway National Recreation Area in 1972. Although the field is no longer an active airport, it serves the community in a variety of ways. The administration building, flight tower, and runways are preserved as historic landmarks and are listed on the National Register of Historic Sites. Hangars used by the U.S. Navy during World War II are used by the New York City Police Helicopter Squadron, the

Floyd Bennett Field was an aviation hub in the 1930s and 1940s.

Parks Commission, and other agencies. The Ryan Visitor Center is named after Congressman William Fitz Ryan, who provided impetus to the act of Congress that created Gateway. The center offers a variety of concession activities and aviation history displays and contains offices for park administration.

A large parcel of open land has been set aside for community gardens, with plots assigned to applicants on a lottery basis. On weekends and summer evenings dozens of local residents come to Floyd Bennett to tend their crops of tomatoes, squash, lettuce, and other vegetables.

A section of runway has been converted to a model airplane flight center, complete with a meteorological station.

Some of the most important programs at Floyd Bennett Field involve natural history and environmental education. They include reintroduction of native grasslands, construction of freshwater ponds and hiking trails, natural history seminars, and a native plant propagation program. Floyd Bennett Field is home to the New York City Board of Education's Gateway Environmental Study Center, a hands-on teacher training center that uses Gateway environments as laboratories to study nature and ecology.

Today, model airplane enthusiasts are the only pilots who prepare their crafts for flight from Floyd Bennett Field.

Grassland Restored

In colonial days, horseback riders traveling through Brooklyn, Queens, and Nassau Counties would get their breeches wet from dew off the grasses. But the vast Hempstead Plains grasslands of colonial times have largely been taken over by development; by the early 1990s only about 19 acres of the original grassland remained on Long Island. Visitors to Floyd Bennett Field today can get an idea of what the Hempstead grasslands were like, however. Grasses may never again cover much of Brooklyn, Queens, and Nassau Counties, as they did in the early 1700s, but the 140 acres of grasses at Floyd Bennett Field provide a bit of botanical history. And the grasses are important not only from a botanical point of view, but for birds and other wildlife as well.

The grasslands were an important habitat for several species of birds, and when the grasses disappeared, the birds left also. The grass-restoration project has helped the bird population rebound. Once again, grasshopper sparrows and other species are nesting in the grasslands of the old airfield.

Through plantings and natural colonization, the park has reestablished stands of mixed grasses, common reed, shrub thickets of bayberry and winged sumac, and scattered stands of black cherry, gray birch, and cottonwood.

Left alone, most grasslands naturally revert to forest as the shrubs and trees invade and begin to shade out the grasses below. In the natural scheme of things, the occasional wildfire removes the shrubs and trees, and the grasses then return. With the decline of grassland habitat in the northeastern United States—partly from fire suppression, mostly from development—a number of grassland birds had been listed by many states as endangered, threatened, or of special concern.

The possibility of losing still more grassland habitat at Floyd Bennett Field through natural plant succession led to research of bird-habitat relationships. Even before Gateway's beginnings in 1972, the old airfield had become known for its ability to support populations of breeding and wintering grassland birds; it would be a good place to study the ecological relationships. As a result of the research, a "grassland indicator species," grasshopper sparrow, was identified, and prime habitat was delineated. A resulting habitat-management program now provides for a number of successional stage habitats, thereby maintaining greater species diversity in this revitalized ecosystem.

The restored grasslands at Floyd Bennett Field prompted the return of several bird species and other wildlife that had been edged out by urbanization.

In winter, the short-eared owl is a common inhabitant of the grasslands.

Grassland restoration began in 1985 when park staff and volunteers from the New York City chapter of the Audubon Society began removing trees and shrubs from designated grasslands. The areas are maintained now by mowing and prescription burns. Since the program began, grasshopper sparrows have increased in abundance and have returned to restored areas that were earlier abandoned. Other grassland species that use the areas include northern harrier, common barn owl, short-eared owl, and upland sandpiper.

Hiking the North 40

When you visit Gateway, take a walk along the hiking trails in the North 40 at Floyd Bennett Field: you'd never know you're on an abandoned airport in one of the largest cities in the world. Several trails snake through grassland, shrubs, and woods and bend around a freshwater pond filled with birds most seasons of the year. Two rustic observation blinds provide a close-up view of the waterfowl and shorebirds without disturbing them.

The pond and trails were built in 1989, complementing other restoration and interpretive programs at Floyd Bennett Field. Funding from the New York State Department of Environmental Conservation was provided largely through the generosity of New York taxpayers who checked off the return-a-gift-to-wildlife block on their tax returns. With volunteer help the trail was built in the most remote section of the airfield—thus the name North 40—and took advantage of existing natural features, such as a wide range of plant succession and an upland area that retained pooled water most of the year. Volunteers also helped build a pond and construct the two blinds. Interpretive signs and a kiosk at the entrance make the trail self-guiding.

The North 40 has become an oasis for wildlife and for birders and hikers alike. The thickets provide food and shelter for many species of resident and migratory birds. Warblers pass through in spring and fall, and the rufous-sided towhee, whose numbers are declining in the Northeast, is among the residents.

By encouraging diversity of habitat, wildlife species using the North 40 have also increased. The protected freshwater pond, just a short flight from Jamaica Bay, is a winter sanctuary for many species of dabbling ducks and Canada geese. In spring and summer glossy ibis can be seen, and mallards, black ducks, and wood ducks build nests in the thickets surrounding the pond. Painted turtles and water snakes can be seen basking on logs. Nesting boxes have been erected for tree swallows, house wrens, and barn owls.

Most of the native plants in the pond area were propagated in the National Park Service greenhouse at Floyd Bennett Field. Major plant communities include sago pondweed, arrowhead, and smartweed. Coontail, mushgrass, and duckweed were planted in the pond; wild millet, crownvetch, birdsfoot trefoil, flatpea, and deertongue were planted on the berms. All play an important role in providing food and protection from predators to wildlife.

Each year, the park's greenhouse yields more than 5,000 plants for habitat restoration projects.

Along the trails, park personnel planted autumn olive, multiflora rose, and red cedar. Butterfly bush and butterfly weed were planted to attract butterfly species. The red cedars and Japanese black pines provide nesting sites and cover for birds.

The North 40 trails are very popular among local birders and hikers, and they are used by some 8,000 schoolchildren each year who participate in the park's Operation Explore Program and Gateway's Ecology Village. Ecology Village was the first regularly utilized overnight camping program within New York City. The young participants have an opportunity to pitch tents, gather vegetables from urban gardens for meals, catch fish from the Bay, prepare campfires, and spend a night under the stars. The program is highly popular with teachers throughout New York City. With just about one million schoolchildren in the New York City Board of Education system, we will always have an audience for the natural events around the North 40 trail and pond.

STATEN ISLAND

The Staten Island unit extends along the south shore of Staten Island and includes Miller Field, Great Kills Park, and Hoffman and Swinburne Islands. Activities include swimming, fishing, boating, jogging, nature study, model airplane flying, picnicking, and organized sports.

Natural habitats include shoreline and dunes; uplands of grasses, shrubs, and small trees; freshwater wetlands; and a locally unique swamp white oak forest.

Miller Field, a former U.S. Army base, has two post–World War I military aircraft hangars, sixty-four acres of athletic fields, picnic areas, a community garden, and the swamp white oak forest. It served as a seaplane base in the years after World War II.

Great Kills Park has a guarded swimming beach, a seasonal food stand, a marina, athletic fields, a public boat ramp, nature trails, a model airplane field, a permit-only fishing area, and several miles of trails for jogging, cycling, and skating.

Great Kills, which faces Lower New York Bay and Raritan Bay, was once the site of an Algonquin village. The topography of the area has changed greatly over the past century, largely because of massive land-filling in the 1940s. Crooke's Point, once Crooke's Island before it was connected by dredged soil to the mainland, is a choice spot for fishing. The center of Crooke's Point is being allowed to return to its natural state and is preserved as a habitat for plants, birds, and other animals. It is a stopping place for monarch butterflies during their migration to Mexico, and butterfly walks are offered during the spring and summer. Bird walks, geology walks, and star watches are also popular at this unit of the park.

Hoffman and Swinburne Islands were constructed in 1872 to serve as a quarantine station and crematorium for immigrants entering the United

Double-crested cormorants nest on the islands off the Staten Island shoreline.

States. Under the administration of the National Park Service since 1974, these islands off the Staten Island coast have become nesting sanctuaries for many native bird species and are not open to the public. Double-crested cormorants, herring, and great black-backed gulls nest on these islands.

Since the U.S. military's downsizing following the end of the Cold War, military facilities and their adjacent lands have been turned over to the National Park Service. On Staten Island the historic Fort Wadsworth lies at the confluence of the Hudson River and Atlantic Ocean and overlooks the Verrazano Bridge and the mouth of New York Harbor; at Great Kills in the Staten Island Unit, the Park Service is constructing a state-of-the-art environmental education center, which opens to the public in 1996.

SANDY HOOK

The Sandy Hook Unit of Gateway National Recreation Area is a narrow peninsula (technically, a sand spit) on the northern tip of the New Jersey shore. To the east is the Atlantic Ocean, and to the west, across a ridge of dunes and leeward salt marsh, is Sandy Hook Bay, separating the peninsula from the New Jersey mainland.

Unlike most of the New Jersey shore, Sandy Hook is virtually undeveloped and boasts some of the most remarkable natural features on the mid-Atlantic coast. An old-growth maritime forest, for example, has an American holly tree documented as more than 150 years old.

Stand on the North Beach of Sandy Hook, and if the skies are reasonably clear, you will see Breezy Point across the waters of New York Harbor to the Rockaway Inlet.

Sandy Hook could be called the southern gatepost of the entrance to New York Harbor, and over the years it has served the New York environs in a number of ways. The original Sandy Hook lighthouse was built in 1764, and it has guided ships into the harbor ever since. It is the oldest operating lighthouse in the United States.

Sandy Hook has played a role in national defense at least since the War of 1812, when the army first built permanent fortifications. Fort Hancock and a series of gun batteries were built in the late 1800s, and they served until 1972, when the fort was decommissioned and transferred to Gateway. Today, many of the buildings of Fort Hancock are used by environmental groups and researchers studying the flora and fauna of this coastal ecosystem.

The U.S. Coast Guard operates its Sandy Hook station on the northern tip of the peninsula, and it is the only remaining active military presence on the hook.

Sandy Hook is of interest to historians, naturalists, birders, fisher-

The lighthouse at Sandy Hook—the oldest beacon still operating in the United States—was built in 1764.

men, swimmers, and others who simply enjoy a somewhat remote seaside environment.

A visit to the Sandy Hook Museum, which includes the original military jailhouse, and to the History House, located in a restored home along Officers' Row, will provide insights into the operation of Fort Hancock. The park visitor center—in the restored U.S. Lifesaving Service station on your right as you enter the park—has many artifacts associated with the Lifesaving Service and beach rescue.

So vital has this peninsula been to the history and culture of the region, and indeed the entire nation, that it has been designated a National Historic Landmark.

The six-and-one-half-mile-long peninsula gets its share of human visitors, especially during the summer, but management practices protect the rich natural habitats of Sandy Hook. In June and July, you'll find crowds of people swimming and working on their tans, but adjacent to them, across a well-marked barrier, there will be endangered piping plovers, least and common terns, black skimmers, and American oystercatchers. In recent years, some thirty-five pairs of plovers have been nesting on the beach, making it one of the most productive plover colonies per acre on the East Coast. Special wire fences built by park personnel protect the nesting birds by eliminating large predators such as raccoons, gulls, and feral cats.

The most important natural asset of Sandy Hook is the maritime forest, which extends along Spermaceti Cove just west of the ranger station, and northwest of the visitor center up to Fort Hancock. Here you can find the American holly tree, wild black cherry, and eastern red cedar. A trail begins at an overlook on the south side of the forest and then winds through a high marsh, a shrub thicket, and finally through the grove of hollies. Ranger-led walks are provided.

Some of the trees are more than 100 years old, and although their trunks are massive, the upper limbs have been pruned and twisted by prevailing winds and the many storms that have buffeted this barrier island environment. The holly is a hardy plant, however, and it has adapted well to the sandy soil, salt air, and occasional northeaster.

Perhaps the greatest danger to this maritime forest came around the turn of the century, when locals would come to the hook to cut holly trees for Christmas decorations. As the number of holly cutters increased—and perhaps as a market for holly became established on the mainland—the trees became endangered. Because the forest was a government reservation, the army at Fort Hancock intervened, posting guards at the holly forest prior to the holiday season.

The holly forest is a unique and valuable natural resource. It is the only such stand remaining in the region, and the trees are popular with many species of birds, which nest among the thick, spiked leaves and feed on the red berries. The forest has been recommended for inclusion in the Department of the Interior's National Natural Landmarks program.

The hollies also have a thick understory of greenbrier, poison ivy, virginia creeper, and honeysuckle, and this thicket is home to a wide variety of birds and animals. Look closely at the dead tree trunks of holly and you might just see an opossum nesting in a cavity.

The holly forest and other areas of Sandy Hook are the focus of organized tours led by park naturalists. The best way to see and appreciate these areas is to accompany someone who is familiar with the flora and fauna and history of the area. Details are available at the visitor center or at any Gateway facility.

If you can't join an organized tour, the next best thing would be a self-guided hike along the Old Dune Trail, a one-mile loop that will introduce you to most of the plants of Sandy Hook, and to other attractions, natural and otherwise. A self-guiding brochure is available at the visitor center.

The trail begins at the parking area of the visitor center, progresses northward, and crosses the primary dunes to end up at the ocean. On the way, you'll see bayberry, prickly pear cactus, junipers, sumac, poison ivy, holly, black cherry, and shadbush, among many other plants. The brochure also points out damage by the human hand, in this case dunes destroyed by bulldozers when a parking lot was built.

Along the trail, expect to see a variety of birds; perhaps a cottontail rabbit, opossum, or raccoon; and reptiles, amphibians, and waterfowl at the freshwater pond. Among the more unusual, and somewhat sinister, way points are the Nike missile sites of the 1950s; the "roads leading nowhere," which actually did lead to ammunition dumps during the Cold War years; and a host of depressions that are craters formed when the hook was utilized as a proving ground by the U.S. Navy in the early 1900s.

The primary human activities at Sandy Hook include swimming, fishing, and nature study. Parking lots are convenient to the ocean beach and to several bayside coves as well. Fishing is good on either side of the peninsula. Flounder and weakfish can be taken in Horseshoe Cove, Spermaceti Cove, and Sandy Hook Bay. A wide variety of fish, depending upon the season, are available to surf fishermen. Ask for a fisheries flyer, which lists those common fish species you can catch or see at Gateway.

FLORA

A diversity of animals requires a diversity of vegetation and habitat. Much of Gateway has undergone major landform changes because of filling and dredging, as well as development up to most of the park's boundary. Yet visitors to Gateway during the annual spring bloom will be pleasantly surprised. They can see, for example, the regional native cactus species in full bloom, as I did on my first walk through the holly forest at the Sandy Hook unit of Gateway over twenty years ago. Brilliant yellow flowers against the cactus green and sand buff colors revealed a desert environment right here in the Northeast.

Crooke's Point Natural Area in the Staten Island unit's Great Kills District provides a refreshing look at bygone days. Vehicles are allowed only by permit, so bring your walking shoes for a glimpse of the shy woodcock and the dunes, which are in bloom from early spring to late fall. Launch your boat from the boat ramp and enjoy the quiet waters around Staten Island as you look back to the landforms of the harbor. For more strenuous activity use the ball fields at Miller field or enjoy a walk in the swamp white oak forest.

At Floyd Bennett Field in Jamaica Bay the North 40 pond has an assortment of freshwater plant species ranging from deep-water submergents to shallow-water emergents. Sago pondweed (*Potamogeton pectinatus*), arrowhead (*Sagittaria latifolia*), and smartweed (*Polygonum pennsylvanicum*) are major components. On the berms, ground cover such as wild millet (*Echinochloa crus-galli*) and birdsfoot trefoil (*Lotus corniculatus*) is grown from cuttings and seeds started in the park's greenhouse. Nest boxes, native animal releases, and planting to attract insects are all part of the North 40 pond action plan.

Walking the shoreline and upland areas of the park will be interesting as you try to identify plants along trails or walkways. Remember,

37

though, that plants may not be collected. Observe all signs so as to protect the natural spaces in the park.

NORWAY SPRUCE (*Picea abies*)

Description. A species introduced during early colonial times, this
evergreen tree has naturalized itself throughout the park. Foliage ranges
from spruce green to deep blue. Spruce needles are short, stiff, and tightly
arranged along branches, giving the tree a neat appearance.

Distribution. Adapted well to colder temperatures and exposed sites,
spruces are found as single specimens and group colonies.

Remarks. Their slow growth provides excellent cover for overwinter-
ing songbirds. They make good windbreak trees and are the most popular
Christmas trees. Have large cones.

EASTERN WHITE PINE (*Pinus strobus*)

Description. Tallest evergreen pine species found in Gateway NRA.
Its blue-green, fragrant needles are found in bundles of five and are soft
to the touch. White pines grow fast. The tree has a pyramidal shape with
whorls of horizontal branches and elongated cones.

Distribution. Found growing throughout Gateway. A large, mature
stand exists on Floyd Bennett Field.

Remarks. White pines are a valuable timber species in the Northeast. They produce cones at an early age and, therefore, colonize an area
in a monoculture. The beauty of this native pine has made it a good can-
didate for several white pine cultivars that are grown for commercial use.

JAPANESE BLACK PINE (*Pinus thunbergii*)

Description. Coniferous tree with green or yellow flowers. Blooms in
April and May. An evergreen, it provides cover for birds and mammals.
Owls, nuthatches, mourning doves, robins, squirrels, and crossbills fre-
quent these trees.

Distribution. Found in dune, landscape, and woodland areas.

Remarks. This alien species thrives in coastal (high-salt) environments. It was planted throughout the park during the military phases
of Gateway's history and extensively under Lady Bird Johnson's "Plant

a Tree in America" program. This tree is the major windbreak for the park's campsites and picnic areas.

EASTERN RED CEDAR (*Juniperus virginiana*)

Description. Native coniferous tree. Flowers in May, June, and July. Blooms are green or yellow. Bluish, fragrant berries in fall. The heartwood is aromatic and rose-brown.

Distribution. Found on dunes, in shrub thickets, and in woodlands.

Remarks. The seeds pass intact through birds' digestive tracts and are then dropped at perching sites. Bobwhites, sharp-tailed grouse, pheasants, mourning doves, and opossums consume the fruits. Provides nesting cover for robins, finches, and mockingbirds, as well as roosting sites for saw-whet owls. Wood is used for cedar chests.

AMERICAN BEACHGRASS (*Ammophila breviligulata*)

Description. The most common grass found growing along the dune areas, it reaches a height of two to four feet. It grows in clumps and is chiefly responsible for the stabilization of beach environments. Spike-

American beachgrass

shaped seed heads that form in August are approximately six inches long and are straw colored.

Distribution. Grows in sandy areas and bluffs in coastal and brackish environments.

Remarks. *Ammophila*'s spreading ability is due to creeping rhizomes that stabilize the shifting sand dunes. This grass has been successfully transplanted throughout the park. It is very sensitive to foot and tire traffic, so please do not walk on dunes unless there is a bridge or trail to follow.

REED GRASS (*Phragmites australis*)

Description. Tall perennial grass that provides a buffer around fresh and brackish marshes. Purple flowers bloom from May through September. Plumelike clusters of seeds.

Distribution. Found on dunes and in disturbed areas throughout the park.

Remarks. Spreads vigorously by underground stems. Forms dense stands along marshes. The fronds of this plant were used by Europeans as thatch for roofs. Fires in large *"Phrag"* stands can be very intense; no-smoking rules are strictly enforced in the park.

LITTLE BLUESTEM (*Andropogon scoparius*)

Description. Native perennial grass. Color varies from yellow to orange (in winter) to green. Juncos and sparrows pluck off the feathery part and eat the seeds within.

Distribution. Found on dunes and in disturbed areas and grasslands. Grows well in dry, sandy soil.

Remarks. Also known as bunchgrass. Gets its common name from color of the stem bases, which are bluish in spring.

SALT MARSH GRASS (*Spartina alterniflora*)

Description. Found growing along tidal banks and creeks, this flat grass is inundated during high tide. Flower spikes are present in midsummer, with tiny, whitish inflorescences.

Distribution. Found growing in the intertidal area along protected bays and channels.

Remarks. Spartina is the primary vegetative matter that supplies the marine estuary ecosystem, as its abundance is the main component of the detritus in the marine food web. Many marine species and shorebirds find cover and nesting areas among this tall grass. Special plant tissue has the ability to extract salt from the surrounding bay waters. Run your fingers along the bottoms of the leaves and see the salt crystals on your skin.

SALT MEADOW HAY (*Spartina patens*)

Description. Occurs along the upland foredunes as a common clump of growing grass. Since salt hay is finer than both marsh grass and beach grass, the grass leaves are less resistant to wind and often roll up. The grass clumps appear windblown and mat over. Seed heads form in midsummer.

Distribution. Grows in protected intertidal bay areas around the park. Salt meadow hay is very tolerant of salt water and is the first true grass to invade low, exposed sandy areas.

Remarks. Salt meadow hay produces a large amount of seeds. Colonial settlers allowed their cattle to graze this grass. It provides good winter cover for small animals.

COTTONWOOD (*Populus deltoides*)

Description. This native deciduous tree has white or green flowers in May. Trees may reach a height of 100 feet or more.

Distribution. Found in dune, disturbed, woodland, or landscaped areas. Also grows in moist soil along streams.

CRACK WILLOW (*Salix fragilis*)

Description. Has broad crown of upright branches and glossy yellow-green twigs. Fine-toothed, bright green leaves.

Distribution. Found in the swamp white oak forest and at the Sandy Hook unit.

NORTHERN BAYBERRY (*Myrica pensylvanica*)

Description. Native shrub or small tree that has yellow or green flowers. Blooms in April and May. Berries have a waxy coating. Yellow-rumped warblers live on the berries during winter.

Distribution. Found on dunes and in disturbed still areas.

Remarks. Has pleasing scent. This plant was used by colonists to make candles.

BLACK WALNUT (*Juglans nigra*)

Description. Large shade tree with deeply grooved bark. Leaves have oval, toothed leaflets. Fruit is a round shell enclosing an irregular nut that is eaten by mice and squirrels.

Distribution. Found in the swamp white oak forest and at the Sandy Hook unit.

EUROPEAN BLACK ALDER (*Alnus glutinosa*)

Description. Dark, striped bark and round-oval double-toothed leaves. Small, white flowers bloom from March through May. Small, conelike fruit with scales on long, thin stalk. Seeds are flat and margined with a papery wing and are eaten by siskins, goldfinches, and redpolls.

Distribution. Found in the swamp white oak forest and at the Sandy Hook unit.

Remarks. Provides a cover for wildlife.

GRAY BIRCH (*Betula populifolia*)

Description. Small, native deciduous tree with chalky white bark marked with dark chevrons and horizontal lines. Has triangular double-toothed leaves. Flowers bloom in April and May and fruits arrive in September. Hardy and can withstand smog and dirt. Green or yellow flowers. These trees are the first to colonize in disturbed areas, such as those dominated by marsh reeds.

Distribution. Woodlands and disturbed and landscaped areas.

Remarks. Common pioneer species, popularly thought to resemble paper birch.

WHITE OAK (*Quercus alba*)

Description. Tall tree with large, lateral branches and a spreading crown. Leaves are broad at the tip and narrow at the base with blunt lobes. Acorns are in scaly cups.

Distribution. Found in the swamp white oak forest, at the Sandy Hook unit, and on Floyd Bennett Field.

SWAMP WHITE OAK (*Quercus bicolor*)

Description. Leaves have very shallow lobes and blunt teeth. Oval acorns are usually in pairs with long stalks.

Distribution. This tree grows in moist soil and is noted as a bottom land tree because of high soil moisture requirements. There is a forest of swamp white oak at the Staten Island unit.

PIN OAK (*Quercus palustris*)

Description. Fast-growing oak that thrives better in moist locations than other oaks. Has tiers of branches that bear leaves with deep lobes and small, round acorns.

Distribution. Found in the swamp white oak forest at the Staten Island unit.

WILLOW OAK (*Quercus phellos*)

Description. Native deciduous tree that has inconspicuous green or yellow flowers in April and May.

Distribution. Found in woodlands, freshwater marshes, and landscaped areas. New York State is northern limit of range. Some planted at the Jamaica Bay Wildlife Refuge.

Remarks. Used by squirrels to make nests.

NORTHERN RED OAK (*Quercus rubra*)

Description. The top of this tall tree is usually rounded. Leaves have toothed lobes. Acorns are oval with a flat, saucerlike cup at the base.

Distribution. Found in the swamp white oak forest at the Staten Island unit.

BLACK OAK (*Quercus velutina*)

Description. Large tree with dark green, sharp-pointed, bristle-tipped leaves with lobes. Has acorns that are oval or egg shaped.

Distribution. Found in the swamp white oak forest at the Staten Island unit.

AMERICAN ELM (*Ulmus americana*)

Description. Large tree whose trunk divides at the base, forming limbs. Leaves are wide ovals. Small, green flowers on drooping stalks bloom from March through May, and small nuts appear in April and May.

Distribution. Found in the swamp white oak forest in the Staten Island unit.

Remarks. Fruit is eaten by foxes, opossums, squirrels, and ground birds.

WHITE MULBERRY (*Morus alba*)

Description. Yellow-brown bark and leaves that are heart shaped or irregularly lobed. An Asiatic tree similar to red mulberry, but leaves are hairless, and buds are red-brown. Fruits, whitish, in September.

Distribution. Found in the swamp white oak forest at the Staten Island unit.

Remarks. Introduced by the British before the American Revolution in an unsuccessful attempt to establish a silkworm industry.

RED MULBERRY (*Morus rubra*)

Description. Small tree with dark, scaly, red-brown bark. Fine-toothed leaves can be either heart shaped or irregularly lobed and turn yellow in autumn. Red or purple berries appear in June and July.

Distribution. Found throughout the park.

Remarks. Common tree of dry, disturbed soil. Fruits are favored by many birds, insects, and small mammals.

GLASSWORT (*Salicornia virginica*)

Description. This native herb can be found in disturbed areas, salt marshes, and dunes. The green or white flowers bloom from July to September. In fall it turns red-orange. Has creeping succulent stems that form extensive mats holding water.

Distribution. Along coastlines in high marshes.

Remarks. After a high tide in fall as the *Salicornia* exhibits its brilliant red color, the glistening plants coated with water are truly a beautiful sight.

BOUNCING BET (*Saponaria officinalis*)

Description. This low-growing perennial has opposite, narrow, fleshy leaves. Its pale pink flowers form a cluster on top of the forb in June.

Distribution. Found in open areas and fields throughout the park. Grows in patches and uniform stands.

Remarks. Bouncing bet is also commonly called soapwort. The colonists used the root of this plant as a natural soap.

JAPANESE BARBERRY (*Berberis thunbergii*)

Description. Low oriental shrub with wedge-shaped leaves that turn scarlet in the fall. Bright red fruits are eaten by pheasant, bobwhite, and grouse. Yellow flowers bloom in April and May.

Distribution. Found throughout the park.

Remarks. Common hedge that escapes to grasslands and open field areas.

SASSAFRAS (*Sassafras albidum*)

Description. Tree with irregular, elliptical leaves that may have two or three lobes. Small green-yellow flowers bloom in April and May. Blue fruit appears from April to May.

Distribution. Found in the swamp white oak forest at the Staten Island unit.

Remarks. Popular plant for spicebush swallowtail butterfly.

SEA ROCKET (*Cakile edentula*)

Description. This pioneer plant species is found just beyond the intertidal area. This hardy succulent is yellowish green with opposite and slightly toothed leaves. Small, pale lavender flowers found on the terminal tips of branches in July.

Distribution. Found growing on natural bluffs in sandy, open environs.

Remarks. Sea rocket gets its name from its uniquely shaped seed capsule. Resembling a rocket, this two-compartment setup allows the top seed to pop and float off or blow away to grow in another area while the lower seed remains near the parent plant. Sea rocket leaves are edible and have a sharp mustard taste.

SWEETGUM (*Liquidambar styraciflua*)

Description. Tall tree has grooved, grayish bark and stubby spur branches and grows in cool, moist woods. Leaves are star shaped. Flowers in spherical heads bloom in April and May. Fruit is a brown, dry, prickly ball appearing from September to November.

Distribution. Found in the swamp white oak forest in the Staten Island unit.

SHADBLOW OR SERVICEBERRY (*Amelanchier canadensis*)

Description. Small deciduous tree that ranges from twelve to twenty feet in height. Naturalized throughout Gateway NRA. The tree produces white, fluffy blooms in the early spring that give the tree a billowy appearance. The summer leaves are silvery green, elliptical, and slightly toothed. The blue-black berries are favored by songbirds.

Distribution. Found in all units of Gateway, often comprising two very different habitats: low, spreading dense thickets as well as low, rounded tree stands.

Remarks. The fruits of serviceberries are often referred to as juneberries because they ripen in June and are an uncommon treat to both wildlife and people. One of the first trees to flower in spring.

HAWTHORN (*Crataegus* genus)

Description. Native trees and shrubs. Displays white or pink flowers from April through June, followed by fruit.

Distribution. Found in woodland and landscaped and shrub thickets, where birds use its dense branches for nesting. Widespread group. Fruit, which remains on plants all year, is eaten by birds and small mammals.

Remarks. Frequent hybridization complicates species identification.

Beach plum

BEACH PLUM *(Prunus maritima)*

Description. Low-growing mounding shrub three to four feet in height. Has deep reddish brown branches, with white striations common to members of the cherry family. Beach plums bloom in late spring, with white flowers that turn pale pink. The reddish purple plums are one inch in circumference and follow in June.

Distribution. Well-drained sandy sites. Beach plums are found in dune and bluff areas throughout Gateway.

Remarks. Quite adaptable, this shrub seems to welcome the constant build-up and depletion of sand common to the seaside environment. Its extensive taproot system allows one mature plant to extend thirty inches in width. Jellies made from the plums have found their way to the finest gourmet stores.

Black cherry

BLACK CHERRY *(Prunus serotina)*

Description. Native deciduous tree with white flowers that bloom in April and May and attract bees and butterflies. Rough outer bark with horizontal lines shows a red-brown underbark when cracked. White flowers bloom in May and June, and fruits are seen from June through October.

Distribution. Found in woodland, dune, disturbed, and shrub thicket areas. Also found in the swamp white oak forest at the Staten Island unit.

Remarks. Common pioneer species. One of the largest cherries, its wood is used by humans for furniture. Songbirds, grouse, rabbits, and gray squirrels regularly consume the fruits. When the berries ferment, it's a sight to see the birds react!

MULTIFLORA ROSE *(Rosa multiflora)*

Description. This perennial shrub is one of the tallest roses. Small clusters of flowers bloom in July and August, and round, red fruit is eaten by birds.

Distribution. Found in woodland, disturbed areas, and freshwater marshes. Also found in the swamp white oak forest at the Sandy Hook unit.

Remarks. Sold as a hedge in nurseries. Provides cover for wildlife. Planted during the restoration of disturbed sites throughout the park. After the red rose hips develop, mockingbirds will claim the area and use them as a winter food source.

SALT SPRAY ROSE (*Rosa rugosa*)

Description. A rounded shrub reaching four feet and found in open sandy environments. This introduced species has glossy, wrinkled leaves with spiny, hairy branches. Red-orange rose hips form in August.

Distribution. Found on dunes and in upland environments throughout Gateway.

Remarks. *Rosa rugosa* forms an impenetrable thicket cover for birds, mice, and rabbits. The rose hips are a source of vitamin C and were used by colonists for jellies and tea. Because of the beneficial qualities of this shrub, it has been propagated and planted throughout the park. Many cultivars were used, each providing a different season of bloom as well as flower color. Cultivars include 'Hansa' (double pink), 'Sir Thomas Lipton' (double white), 'Persian Yellow' (double yellow), and 'Austrian Copper' (deep copper).

BLACKBERRY (*Rubus allegheniensis*)

Description. Shrub grows in thickets and has angular stems with thorns. White flowers bloom from May through June, and fruits appear from July to September.

Distribution. Found in the swamp white oak forest and at the Sandy Hook unit.

AILANTHUS (*Ailanthus altissima*)

Description. Crushed leaves emit a strong odor, giving the tree its common name, tree of heaven. Green or yellow flowers appear in early summer.

Distribution. Found throughout the park.

Remarks. Common tree of urban areas; found on many New York City streets.

WINGED SUMAC (Rhus copallina)

Description. Shrub with compound leaves of smooth-edged leaflets. Red, hairy fruit is eaten by birds, and rabbits eat the twigs.

Distribution. Found in the swamp white oak forest at the Staten Island unit.

POISON IVY (Rhus radicans)

Description. Deciduous vine or shrub. Small, yellow flowers bloom from May through July, and small, greenish white, round fruit clusters appear from August through November. Characteristic clusters of three leaves.

Distribution. Found encasing holly, among other trees, in all areas of the park.

Remarks. Many people are allergic to the oils of this plant. As a rule, stay away from vines with "leaves of three," since this is a good indication of poison ivy. The berries are a significant source of food for songbirds, and the denser shrub areas are used for ground cover by birds and mammals.

INKBERRY (Ilex glabra)

Description. Evergreen woodland shrub that is a member of the holly family. Has smooth green leaves and black berries.

Distribution. Found in Fort Tilden, Jamaica Bay District, and the Jamaica Bay Wildlife Refuge.

Remarks. Prefers moist yet well-drained soil. Generally, shaded woodland areas are its home. Provides nesting and cover for songbirds. Fruits are food for many songbirds and wild turkey. Another common name is low gallberry holly.

AMERICAN HOLLY (Ilex opaca)

Description. Native coniferous tree that reaches a height of 100 feet. Along the seashore they are stunted in height by sea winds and breezes.

Leaves are spiny and scalloped. Female trees bear bright red, glossy berries in winter.

Distribution. Holly trees do well in woodland and dune areas. Sandy Hook is the home of a maritime forest, where the holly trees thrive in the sandy soil. Sandy Hook's holly forest is being considered for national natural landmark status by the U.S. Department of the Interior.

Remarks. Trees are either male or female, with only female trees producing berries. The spiny leaves are extremely thick, to protect these seaside trees from the salt in the ocean winds. Holly trees provide excellent winter cover for many species of birds and mammals.

BOX ELDER (Acer negundo)

Description. Opposite compound leaves with toothed or lobed, bright green leaflets. Green-yellow flowers bloom in April. Winged seeds appear in September and October.

Distribution. Found in moist soil along streams, and in the swamp white oak forest and at the Sandy Hook unit.

Remarks. Less commonly used name, ashleaf maple, indicates its relationship to the maples. Syrup can be made from its sap. Squirrels and songbirds eat the seeds.

RED MAPLE (Acer rubrum)

Description. Native deciduous tree. Twigs are covered with tiny red flowers in March and April. Paired seeds ripen in the late spring.

Distribution. Found in woodland areas like those near the East Pond at the Jamaica Bay Wildlife Refuge. Grows rapidly in moist, swampy soil. Also found in the swamp white oak forest on Staten Island and at the Sandy Hook unit.

Remarks. Provides food, cover, and nesting sites for wildlife. This species is one of the standard plants that denote wetland (freshwater) boundaries.

SUGAR MAPLE (Acer saccharum)

Description. Leaves have three to five lobes. Clusters of long-stemmed, yellow flowers develop with leaves in April. Paired seeds with U-shaped wings ripen in fall.

Distribution. Found in the swamp white oak forest and at the Sandy Hook unit.

Remarks. The sap from this tree is used to make maple sugar and maple syrup. One of the most valuable hardwood trees, the sugar maple is a source for lumber nationwide.

VIRGINIA CREEPER *(Parthenocissus quinquefolia)*

Description. Climbing vine with tendrils. Leaves have five oblong, toothed leaflets. Small, greenish clusters of flowers bloom from June through August, and blue-black berries appear from August to February.

Distribution. Found in the swamp white oak forest, at the Sandy Hook unit, at Floyd Bennett Field, and in the wildlife refuge.

Remarks. This plant grows extremely well in harsh environments—those that are hot and dry, with nutrient-depauperate soils. On a recent trip to Greece I found it growing on a trellis in a small restaurant on the island of Lindos. Remarkably adaptive plant.

FOXGRAPE *(Vitis labrusca)*

Description. Dark-stemmed, thornless vine with tendrils opposite each leaf. Leaves are long, dark green, and smooth on top, red and woolly underneath. Flowers bloom from May through July, and dark fruits appear from August to October.

Distribution. Found in the swamp white oak forest at the Staten Island unit.

BEACH HEATHER *(Hudsonia tomentosa)*

Description. This prostrate bluish gray plant with needlelike foliage has bright, tiny yellow flowers in June.

Distribution. Found growing in a monoculture in low-lying sandy beach environments and protected areas park wide.

Remarks. This plant assures its development by releasing a slightly toxic substance within its root zone to discourage germination of other plants. This allows for an extensive mat-forming system to develop.

Beach heather

PRICKLY PEAR CACTUS (*Opuntia humifusa*)

Description. Perennial native cactus found on dunes and in salt marshes. Beautiful yellow flower. Grows in clumps or is mat-forming.

Distribution. Found throughout the park; particularly abundant in the Sandy Hook unit along holly forest trails.

Remarks. Only widespread cactus in the eastern United States.

RUSSIAN OLIVE (*Elaeagnus angustifolia*)

Description. A deciduous tree that blooms in May and June. Unlike the autumn olive, the berries of the Russian olive are silvery and bitter tasting. Somewhat thorny. Leaves long and thorny.

Distribution. Disturbed and landscaped areas and shrub thickets from Maine to New Jersey.

Remarks. *Elaeagnus* species are among the few nonlegumes that fix nitrogen in the soil by means of bacterial root nodules.

SILVERBERRY (*Elaeagnus commutata*)

Description. This shrub is related to autumn and Russian olive. Small yellow flowers bloom in September and attract monarch butterflies, bees, and other insects.
Distribution. Disturbed and landscaped areas.
Remarks. Blooms late in season; strongly scented flowers.

AUTUMN OLIVE (*Elaeagnus umbellata*)

Description. Deciduous woodland tree with yellow-white flowers and red berries. Blooms in May and June. Can withstand extreme weather.
Distribution. Can be found in all units of Gateway. Of oriental origin. Sometimes planted for erosion control and ornamental purposes.

SOUR GUM (*Nyssa sylvatica*)

Description. Tall, native shade tree with horizontal branches that droop at the ends. Oval leaves turn red in autumn. Greenish flowers bloom in May and June, followed by dark fruit.
Distribution. Found in the swamp white oak forest in the Staten Island unit.
Remarks. Fleshy, bitter fruits are relished by many species of birds.

EVENING PRIMROSE (*Oenothera biennis*)

Description. A native perennial with alternate narrow leaves reaching three feet in height. In midsummer this forb goes into bloom with four-petal yellow flowers opening in a random fashion along a tan stem.
Distribution. Found growing in sandy, sunny, open areas and along roadsides throughout the park.
Remarks. Its common name comes from the fact that the plant flowers open at dusk and close in bright sunlight. The pointed seedpods are a winter favorite of goldfinches.

QUEEN ANNE'S LACE (*Daucus carota*)

Description. A biennial plant that has leaves similar to the carrot. It produces a white disk bloom with a dark center in late summer through fall. As the flat bloom fades, it shrivels and looks like a tiny bird nest.

Distribution. Found growing in open and upland fields. An excellent pioneer species that has populated most roadways.

Remarks. A common forb, this plant was named for its dainty florets, which resemble fine lace worn by Queen Anne.

SEA LAVENDER (*Limonium carolinianum*)

Description. Perennial forb with a fleshy, basal rosette of large, leathery leaves. Inundated with salt and brackish water, this plant gives rise to a delicate open bouquet of tiny lavender-blue flowers in late fall.

Distribution. Found growing in protected intertidal areas and along channels with little or no wave action.

Remarks. Collected flowers of sea lavender make excellent dried arrangements. A true treasure found growing among the glasswort. Cattle grazed on both species in colonial times.

GREEN ASH (*Fraxinus pennsylvanica*)

Description. Bark is closely furrowed. Flowers bloom in April and May, and fruit appears in early fall.

Distribution. Lowland tree found along stream banks and flood plains. Found in the swamp white oak forest at the Staten Island unit.

BUTTERFLY BUSH (*Buddleia davidii*)

Description. This bush has large, fragrant purple flowers that bloom in the summer and attract many species of butterflies.

Distribution. Parkwide. Has been a major habitat enhancer planted to help attract butterflies.

Remarks. There is a butterfly bush beside the park's greenhouse on Floyd Bennett Field where visitors can observe red admirals, painted ladies, and monarchs feeding on the nectar.

MILKWEED (*Asclepias syriaca*)

Description. A perennial plant with a thick stem and oblong opposite leaves. It blooms in late summer, with globular-shaped flowers that are purplish pink and found along the top. The plant produces a large (four-inch) seedpod that has a horny covering that splits open in fall and emits hundreds of seeds attached to silken threads for flight.

Distribution. Found growing throughout the park in open areas in both dry, sandy soil and moist, poorly drained soil.

Remarks. Several species of milkweed grow in the park. The common milkweed is an important nectar plant for the monarch butterfly, which both feeds and lays her eggs on this plant. The milky sap was used by the settlers to remove warts. The pods, flowers, and stalks were all eaten by the New York Indians.

MULLEIN (*Verbascum* species)

Description. A naturalized biennial, this plant forms a low rosette with large woolly leaves the first year. As the plant matures the rosette gives rise to a thick stem five feet tall, and the top two feet of the plant are covered with cup-shaped yellow flowers in a tightly arranged head.

Distribution. Grows in open areas and along roadsides. Thrives in full sun and is found in all areas of Gateway.

Remarks. Mullein has quite an interesting history. The tall stalks were dried and burned as torches. Traditional herbalists praise this plant's ability to heal respiratory ailments.

JAPANESE HONEYSUCKLE (*Lonicera japonica*)

Description. Woody vine introduced from Asia. Often seen growing at the base of the cottonwood trees. It has a fragrant white or yellow flower.

Distribution. Can be seen in Sandy Hook, Breezy Point, and the Jamaica Bay Wildlife Refuge.

Remarks. Has a particularly lovely fragrance (especially as evening temperatures drop) that attracts insects. Berries are eaten by birds and mice.

MORROW HONEYSUCKLE (*Lonicera morrowii*)

Description. Vine with narrow, gray leaves that are hairy underneath. White or yellow flowers bloom from April through June, followed by red or yellow fruit.

Distribution. Found in the swamp white oak forest at the Staten Island unit.

Remarks. White flowers turn yellow with age.

ELDERBERRY (*Sambucus nigra*)

Description. Shrub with brittle branches. Compound leaves with seven tapering, toothed leaflets. Flowers bloom in small clusters during June.

Distribution. Found in swamps, as well as in the swamp white oak forest and at the Sandy Hook unit.

Remarks. Small purple berries have been used to make wine, jam, and jelly.

ARROWWOOD (*Viburnum dentatum*)

Description. High shrub with coarse-toothed oval leaves. White flowers grow in clusters. Fruit is a dark berry. Hairy twigs.

Distribution. Found in the swamp white oak forest at the Staten Island unit.

Remarks. The northern species *V. recognitum* has fruits eaten by chipmunks. Shoots were used by Native Americans for arrow shafts.

SMOOTH BLACKHAW (*Viburnum prunifolium*)

Description. Native shrub or small deciduous tree with white flowers that bloom in April and May.

Distribution. Found in shrub thickets and landscaped and disturbed areas.

Remarks. This hardy shrub is able to tolerate air pollution. Its berries are food for thrushes, cardinals, pheasants, and squirrels. Used mostly for ornamental plantings.

DUSTY-MILLER (*Artemisia stellerana*)

Description. Low-growing forb with soft greenish white leaves that take on a lobed shape in late fall. Sends up a woody flower stalk, which gives rise to a collection of tiny, rayed yellow blooms.

Dusty-miller

Distribution. Grows in protected, low-lying dune areas and sandy soils.

Remarks. This plant covers over entirely with a white pubescence in winter, giving it added protection from its exposed, harsh environment.

GROUNDSELBUSH *(Baccharis halimifolia)*

Description. This is the tallest shrub found in the transition zone within the intertidal area. Its leaves are succulent, alternating, and toothed. The flowers are cream white to yellow late in July.

Distribution. Found in the upland intertidal areas around Jamaica Bay.

Remarks. Both the pistillate and staminate plants produce flowers, although these are slightly different. A very hardy shrub.

CHICORY *(Cichorium intybus)*

Description. A four-foot-high woody perennial with course, rough leaves. A crisp blue composite flower opens in July.

Distribution. Open fields, roadsides, and sandy areas throughout the park.

Remarks. Chicory seeds are loved by goldfinches. The settlers dried the roots and used them to make a hot beverage as a coffee substitute. Young leaves were also consumed.

GRASSES AND SEDGES: Black Grass (*Juncus gerardi*), Spike Grass (*Desmazeria sicula*), Yellow Nut-Sedge (*Cyperus esculentus*)

Description. Twenty-three species of grasses and sedges grow throughout the park. They do not form clumps and often form uniform stands. Sedges, unlike the grasses, have a triangular stem, giving rise to seed nutlets. The seeds are consumed by numerous birds and small mammals.

MARINE INVERTEBRATES

Any animals without backbones and internal skeletons are considered invertebrates. They predominate the animal world, making up over 95 percent of the known species. Estuarine invertebrates are truly diverse and occupy all habitats along the shore—from mud bottoms to pilings at piers and wharves.

Invertebrates have redirected scientific thought on the early proliferation of life on this planet. Invertebrates were once thought to have been spurred on only by photosynthetic activity, but oceanographers have now discovered chemosynthetic ecosystems at the deep midocean ridges, beyond any light penetration, where active volcanism initiates the sulphur-based processes of life.

This is a small sampling of the more common marine invertebrate species found at Gateway.

COMMON SMOOTH PERIWINKLE (*Littorina littorea*)

Description. The most common northern rock and wharf-piling periwinkle. Up to one and one-quarter inches long. Dull brown to gray.

Distribution. Intertidal; attaches to any solid substratum, such as rocks.

Remarks. Herbivorous. Thought to have been brought to Nova Scotia from western Europe over 100 years ago. Edible after boiling.

BOAT SHELL OR COMMON SLIPPER SHELL (*Crepidula fornicata*)

Description. Shell has platform extending about halfway across opening. This is the "deck" from which shell derives its common names of boat shell and slipper shell.

Distribution. Lower intertidal zone from Gulf of Mexico north to Massachusetts Bay.

Remarks. Found attached to almost any available hard object but especially horseshoe crabs. Hermaphroditic; found in stacks undergoing sex reversals.

MOON SNAIL (*Lunatia heros*)

Description. Gray to tan; up to four inches long. Large, retractable foot. Has open umbilicus. Three to four and one-half inches in length.

Distribution. Deep-water species, to 1,200 feet. Found mostly in sandy shallows.

Remarks. Common on beaches. Sand collars contain their eggs and wash ashore. Very fragile when dried. Prey on other mollusks. Look for their plowed trail in the sandy sediments at low tide.

OYSTER DRILL (*Urosalpinx cinerea*)

Description. Has an open, flaring anterior canal. Adults usually one inch long.

Distribution. Intertidal to subtidal down to about fifty feet in brackish water to minimum salinity of 15 percent.

Remarks. A major predator of oysters; it drills a small hole in the shell and sucks out the oyster.

BLUE MUSSEL (*Mytilus edulis*)

Description. This common smooth-shelled mussel is usually glossy bluish or bluish black. Violet interior. Up to four inches in length.

Distribution. Lower intertidal to subtidal at shallow depths in estuary in slightly brackish water.

Remarks. Mussels compete with barnacles and seaweed to cover intertidal rocks and pilings. They attach themselves by tough threads called byssi. Edible.

ATLANTIC OYSTER (*Crassostrea virginica*)

Description. Extremely variable in shape. Shells are massive, rough, and unequal. Lower valve cements to any hard object available. Young "spats" attach to older oysters, building up extensive mats.

Distribution. Intertidal to subtidal; parkwide in estuary.

Remarks. Many diseases afflict this most edible bivalve. Each female can produce over 100 million eggs per year. Oysters harvested from New York Harbor around the turn of the century were transported all over the world. Oil and bacterial pollution put an end to this commercial industry in New York Harbor.

RIBBED MUSSEL (*Geukensia demissus*)

Description. Oblong, three to four inches, and somewhat pear shaped. Glossy. Yellowish brown to black outside with many ribs. Often rough with fin ribs running lengthwise.

Distribution. Salt marshes and brackish, muddy estuaries. Peat outcroppings.

Remarks. Best seen during low tide, when it is exposed in the marsh grasses. Hardy mussel that is tolerant of extremely high temperatures and saline levels. Found in the mud and attached to *Spartina* stalks in large quantities.

HARD-SHELL OR QUAHOG CLAM (*Mercenaria mercenaria*)

Description. Thick, solid, oval shell. Outside is dull gray; inside is white with purple stain at rear. Young have raised ridges that smooth out as they age.

Distribution. Sand or mud in bays and ocean beaches in shallow water.

Remarks. Commercial names are contingent on the size of the clam. Littlenecks are up to one and a half inches, cherrystones to two inches, and chowder clams to three inches or more. *Quahog* derives from two Narragansett Indian words meaning dark or closed and shell. Its purple and white lining gave it special importance as wampum to prehistoric Native Americans. Clamming in Jamaica Bay is illegal, since benthic invertebrates are the foundation of food webs in the estuary. Commercial clamming is not authorized in Jamaica Bay.

SOFT-SHELL CLAM (*Mya arenia*)

Description. Shells are elongated, thin, and gaping. Surface has rough, wrinkled growth lines. Siphons are fused onto the neck with tough, dark gray skin.

Distribution. Marine and brackish areas. Burrows to ten inches.

Remarks. Also called steamer clam. When disturbed, it spurts water out of a hole in the sand as it retracts its siphon. Undisturbed, at low tide there is a symphony of spraying that so far escapes explanation.

SURF CLAM (*Spisula solidissima*)

Description. Heavy, strong, triangular shell. Smooth surface with fine, concentric lines. Rapid burrower.

Distribution. Found partially embedded in sand near shore on open, exposed beaches like those of Breezy Point. Usually lives in areas with strong waves or rapid tidal current.

Remarks. These clams get washed ashore during winter storms and provide food for the gulls. By dropping the clams onto rocks, the gulls are able to crack them open.

COMMON RAZOR CLAM (*Ensis directus*)

Description. Long, thin, convex, squared ends. Six to ten inches in length.

Distribution. Above low-tide line at sandy shallow bays.

Remarks. This clam can burrow deeply in a short time. Commonly called the Atlantic jackknife clam, its shell does not close at the ends and the animal depends on burrowing for protection. When there are vibrations in the sand covering the clam, the clam's foot protrudes from the lower opening of the valves, swells with blood, and contracts—pulling the clam deeper. Considered by some to be the most delicious clam.

DOG WHELK (*Nassarius obsoletus*)

Description. A dull, dark, weakly sculpted whelk.

Distribution. Chiefly subtidal at shallow depths on mud bottoms. Found all over mudflats; thus sometimes called mud snail.

Remarks. Dog whelks are scavengers and important for recycling dead and decaying materials back into the estuary.

CHANNELED WHELK (*Busycon canaliculatum*)

Description. A large whelk with channeled sutures, or grooves, circulating outside shell. Adults have square-shouldered, distinctive whorls and yellowish aperture. Grows to eight inches.

Distribution. Lower intertidal to subtidal down to sixty feet, along bays and ocean beaches in salinities above 20 percent. Feeds on bivalves.

Remarks. Largest sea snails on the East Coast. Common in shallow water. Strings of their egg capsules are also common along the shoreline.

Channeled whelk egg cases

ROCK BARNACLES (Balanus balanoides)

Description. The common intertidal barnacle along shorelines. White. Found in colonies.

Distribution. Extends subtidally into shallow water but most common intertidally, where it competes with blue mussel and rockweed for space on rocks and pilings.

Remarks. Research on the "glue" of barnacles was important to the U.S. Navy and is studied by the dental industry.

SAND SHRIMP (Crangon septemspinosa)

Description. Transparent, drab, light gray with tiny, irregular black spots. Toothless, short beak.

Distribution. Sandy bottoms and eelgrass beds from low-tide line to water more than 300 feet deep.

Remarks. Common shallow-water species related to prawns.

COMMON SHORE SHRIMP (Palaemonetes vulgaris)

Description. Transparent, slender, and elongated with red, yellow, white, and blue spots on back. Beak tip directed upward.

Distribution. Bays and estuaries from low-tide line to forty-five feet deep.

Remarks. Although transparent, this shrimp contains pigments and has been used to study the hormonal control of color in crustaceans.

BLUE CLAW CRAB (Callinectes sapidus)

Description. Shell more than twice as wide as long. Usually grayish or blue-green, with blue claws and legs. Females have red legs and rounded abdomen. The male's abdomen is tapered.

Distribution. Shallows and brackish estuaries from low tide to 120 feet deep.

Remarks. This species is commercially caught and supports a large seafood industry. Crabbing for this species is also a pastime for visitors; females with eggs, found on the underside, must be returned immediately to water. After these crabs molt, they are called soft-shell crabs.

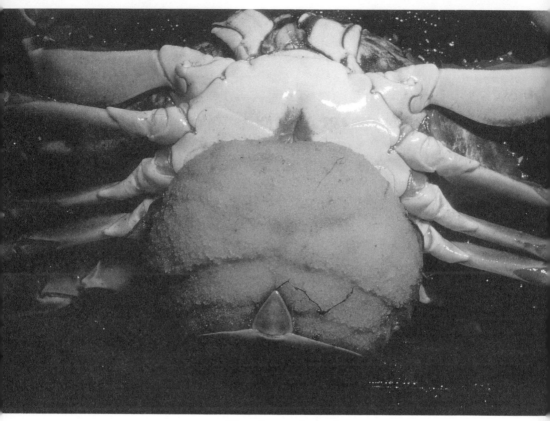

Blue claw crabs with eggs

SPIDER CRAB (*Libinia emarginata*)

Description. Round. Brown to yellowish. Spiny.

Distribution. All types of bottoms, from shoreline in bays and inlets to subtidal at depths of 160 feet.

Remarks. Slow moving and innocuous, despite their appearance. They are often overgrown with algae, sponges, or bryozoans.

FIDDLER CRAB (*Uca pugnax*)

Description. Square shell. Chestnut brown on top. Large pincer. In the male one claw is much larger than the other.

Distribution. Found in muddy marshes and in burrows above the high-tide line.

Spider crab

Fiddler crab

Remarks. Prefers brackish water but can survive for at least three weeks in fresh water. Feeds on organic matter and decaying marsh grass.

ATLANTIC MOLE CRAB (*Emerita talpoida*)

Description. Egg shaped and sand colored. Females are twice the size of males.
Distribution. Open, sandy ocean beaches.
Remarks. Harmless, burrowing crab that digs into the sand at the tide line.

LADY OR CALICO CRAB (*Ovalipes ocellatus*)

Description. Pale grayish crab with minute purple specks in clusters. Last pair of legs is paddle shaped. Grows up to three inches.
Distribution. Found subtidal on sandy bottoms but up to the waterline when tide is in.
Remarks. Buries itself in the sand with eyestalks exposed. Be careful; she's no "lady," but is ill-tempered.

GREEN CRAB (*Carcinus maenas*)

Description. Males and juveniles are chiefly greenish above, yellowish below; adult females are red-orange below and grow to about three inches in width.
Distribution. Intertidal to subtidal at shallow depths.
Remarks. The most common New England shore crab found south of New Jersey to Manasquan Inlet. Introduced from Europe.

HERMIT CRAB (*Pagurus* species)

Description. Small crab that carries a shell in which its unarmored abdomen is concealed. Can leave shell at will.
Distribution. Intertidal to subtidal down to several hundred feet for some species.
Remarks. This crab tightly grips the inside of its borrowed shell, which it changes as it matures.

MUD CRAB (Panopeus herbstii)

Description. Mud colored; claws distinctly unequal; "fingers" black, palms paler. Major claw has a large tooth near base of movable finger.

Distribution. In salinities of 10 percent or more. Most abundant in sponge colonies and intertidal rocks.

Remarks. All mud crabs are important predators of oysters and clams, and their powerful claws can crush a hard-shell clam.

TUBE WORM (Diopatra cupera)

Description. Distinctive projecting tubes encrusted with bits of shell or other debris. Tube is soft but tough. Projects several inches above ground, extending as much as three feet below ground.

Distribution. Intertidal to subtidal.

Remarks. Poking up from tidal mudflats, their chimneys are well camouflaged, resembling stumps of plants.

HORSESHOE CRAB (Limulus polyphemus)

Description. Horseshoe shaped; convex carapace. Spikelike tail, which is harmless. Greenish tan. Males are smaller than females. Related to spiders.

Distribution. Mud or sand bottoms, estuaries.

Remarks. In late spring (last week of May to first week in June) the females lay pale greenish eggs when the tide is high. The male fertilizes the eggs while holding the female. The eggs are then buried in the sand until they hatch. These prehistoric-looking animals, essentially unchanged for more than 200 million years, feed on clams, worms, and other invertebrates.

SAND FLEA (Orchestia platensis)

Description. Semiterrestrial, living at or above upper limit of intertidal zone. Leaps erratically when disturbed. Dark olive to reddish brown.

Distribution. Found on rocky shores or pilings in upper intertidal zone.

Remarks. Common name comes from flealike jumping ability; beach fleas are harmless scavengers. Usually found under dead seaweeds and at the wrack line.

MOONJELLY (*Aurelia aurita*)

Description. Marginal or short tentacles that are very numerous and fringelike. Opaque white or pinkish; translucent whitish gonads, observable. Eight to ten inches across.

Distribution. Spring through summer up to salinities of 16 percent in bays and inlets. Floats on the water's surface.

Remarks. Reportedly less venomous than other jellyfish. Adults feed on small plankters.

COMB JELLY (*Mnemiopis* species)

Description. Body is oval, somewhat flattened, with lobes exceeding body length. Brilliantly luminescent. Up to four inches long.

Distribution. Penetrates the nearly freshwater portions of the estuary parkwide. Year-round, but usually more abundant in late summer.

Remarks. Most common ctenophore south of Cape Cod. Young of a burrowing anemone are parasitic in the gut of comb jellies.

The twin towers of the World Trade Center on the Manhattan skyline present a striking contrast to the Jamaica Bay Wildlife Refuge, a wilderness where the great egret (above) and the great blue heron (right) stop over during migration.

The snowy egret's black bill and yellow feet (obscured here), distinguish it from the great egret, which has a yellow bill and black feet.

Raised platforms, made especially for ospreys to nest in, stand beside John F. Kennedy International Airport on the periphery of East High Meadow Marsh.

Breezy Point, one of the protected beach areas in the park, is a nesting ground for common terns, as well as many other shorebirds, from May until August.

As they fly, black skimmers dip their sharp lower bills into the water to catch fish. These birds nest on the shores of Breezy Point.

Horseshoe crabs congregate on the shores in late spring,
when their mating ritual begins.

Efforts to restore sea-beach amaranth and other endangered plant species are ongoing at Gateway.

Between dives for fish, cormorants perch along the shores of Jamaica Bay, spreading their wings for several minutes to dry their feathers.

Some of the trees in the holly forest on Sandy Hook are more than a hundred years old, having survived many Christmastide snippings before park protection was secured.

The black-throated green warbler is just one of the more than 340 bird species that find sanctuary at Gateway throughout the year.

Visitors can join park-sponsored butterfly walks and spot numerous species, including the tiger swallowtail, which feasts on the nectar of the aptly named butterfly weed.

Monarch butterflies, common in late summer, often gather on the pine trees at Breezy Point.

Once confined to Florida, the glossy ibis is now a common summer resident of Gateway.

In early summer, the female diamondback terrapin leaves the salt marsh for sandy areas to lay her eggs.

The eastern hognose snake has been restored to Gateway by park naturalists.

Spartina alterniflora, *also known as salt marsh cordgrass, has a special membrane that filters harmful salts from the water it takes in, enabling it to thrive in a harsh maritime environment.*

One of the most enchanting times to visit Gateway is in autumn, when the foliage begins to change color.

The only abundant cactus in the eastern United States, the prickly pear cactus with its luminous yellow flowers, is a common sight on Sandy Hook.

The endangered
peregrine falcon
has made a come-
back in recent
years through park
conservation
measures.

The meadow vole,
one of the many
inhabitants of the
fields and grass-
lands, is the most
common mammal
at Gateway.

The grasslands at Floyd Bennett Field are maintained through prescribed burns, which inhibit the spread of shrubs and trees. These burns mimic natural fires set by lightning.

*In winter, the snowy owl can be spotted
in open fields throughout the park.*

FISHES

As part of a 1986 survey of recreational fisheries, a local fisherman casting from a pier in Jamaica Bay was asked, "What do you do with the fish you catch here?" Perplexed by such a simple question, he replied, "I eat it!" That unremarkable yet highly practical answer reflects a unique characteristic of fishing in and at Gateway NRA: people consume what they catch in urban waters. More than 85 percent of the people we surveyed were fishing for food.

Estuaries are important to fisheries because they provide nurseries for young fish to develop, as well as abundant food and shelter for larger fish of prey. Human influences on the estuary have degraded many fish stocks. PCBs in Hudson River striped bass and bluefish have prevented commercial harvesting. New York and New Jersey have issued warnings in recent years against eating bluefish because of high concentrations of PCBs in muscle tissue. In addition, heavy metals from treated wastewater have increased the incidence of bacterial infections in bluefish. The decline in the number of striped bass is due in part to the influence of polycyclic aromatic hydrocarbons (PAHs) and zinc, which have been correlated with reduced reproductive capacity. PCB levels in striped bass tissue, however, have been declining over the last few years.

Jamaica Bay constitutes over half of Gateway National Recreation Area. The bay maintains roles as a nesting area for shorebirds and as a home to many species of fish. A monthly seine is conducted at sampling sites throughout the park, in which fish are counted, identified, measured, and released. Dissolved oxygen, pH, temperature, salinity, and conductivity are also recorded.

This section contains a survey of fish most commonly found in park waters.

Little skate

LITTLE SKATE (*Raja erinacea*)

Description. Has a distinctively blunt snout and three rows of spines along the midline of the back. Tail long and covered with spines.

Distribution. Park waters and shallow surf zones.

Remarks. Lays tough-shelled eggs that contain miniature skates. The cases, which often wash up on the beach, are about two to two and a half inches, are black, and have filaments at each corner.

AMERICAN EEL (*Anguilla rostrata*)

Description. A catadromous (lives in fresh water; goes to sea to spawn), black-blue eel.

Distribution. Bays, estuaries, rivers. Three-year-old larvae drift with currents. Females swim upstream and remain for about eight years before migrating to the ocean.

Remarks. Migrates annually to Sargasso Sea off coast of Africa. Major commercial food. Each female produces as many as twenty million eggs. After the male spreads milt over the eggs, the adults die.

ATLANTIC HERRING (Cluper harengus)

Description. Elongated and silvery with a bluish or greenish blue back; no dark spots.
Distribution. Common north of New Jersey.
Remarks. Valuable fish. Packed as sardines, shipped frozen for bait, and used in the manufacture of oils and fertilizers.

WEAKFISH (Cynoscion regalis)

Description. Dark olive to bluish, with many small dark spots sometimes arranged in diagonal rows.
Distribution. East Coast. Regionally called yellow fin.
Remarks. Name derived from the ease with which a hook can be removed from its mouth. Feeds on sea worms, shrimp, and crabs.

ATLANTIC MENHADEN (Brevoortia tyrannus)

Description. Silvery with brassy sides and a dark, bluish green back. Pale yellowish fins. Adults and large young have numerous spots on side behind the dark shoulder spot. Measures up to fourteen inches.
Distribution. Estuaries.
Remarks. Commonly called bunker or moss bunker on Long Island. Once a viable commercial fish for machine oil and fertilizer, it is now used as a bait fish for bluefish.

OYSTER TOADFISH (Opsanus tau)

Description. Shallow-water marine fish. Dull greenish or brownish. Stout, scaleless body. Very wide mouth. Measures up to eighteen inches.
Distribution. Worldwide.
Remarks. Lays eggs in June; eggs attached by an adhesive disk. Nest guarded by male, who constantly cleans eggs. Feeds on benthic crustaceans and mollusks.

ATLANTIC NEEDLEFISH (*Stringylura mavinus*)

Description. Common, elongated jaws, usually with upper jaw slightly shorter. Band of teeth.

Distribution. Lives primarily in salt water, but will penetrate fresh waters.

Remarks. Travel in schools. As they swim along the surface at night, they may jump at light.

NORTHERN PUFFER (*Sphoarodies maculatus*)

Description. Commonly called blow fish because of its ability to inflate its body with air or water by means of a sac that is an extension of the stomach. Very small mouth; does not have true teeth.

Distribution. Cape Cod to Florida; parkwide at Gateway. Inshore species, yet primarily a bottom feeder.

Remarks. The viscera and skin are toxic and should not be eaten.

NORTHERN SEA ROBIN (*Prionotus carolinus*)

Description. Matted body. Blackish fins. Bony hind. Two to three free lower winglike pectoral fins.

Distribution. Bays and estuaries to 600 feet.

Remarks. The free fins are used for walking along the bottom and as a sense organ. They also produce sound.

SMOOTH DOGFISH (*Mustelus canis*)

Description. Gray or brownish. Small, broadly rounded mouth. Small teeth in rows.

Distribution. Bottom dweller that migrates to deep water during winter.

NORTHERN PIPEFISH (*Syngnathus fuscus*)

Description. Dark body. Mottled with no distinct pattern. Long, thin body. Measures up to twelve inches.

Distribution. Seagrass beds in bays and estuaries.

Remarks. Related to the seahorse. Moves by rapid rippling of the dorsal fin and uses its tail to cling to aquatic plants.

ATLANTIC SILVERSIDE (*Menidia menidia*)

Description. Prominent silver stripe along side. Round belly. Large eyes. Measures up to six inches.

Distribution. Found along sandy seashore and mouths of inlets.

Remarks. Very common throughout Gateway. Can tolerate extreme water temperature but perishes easily when caught in seine net. Popular bait fish for larger game fish. Sold commercially as spearing.

STRIPED KILLIFISH (*Fundulus majalis*)

Description. Male has fifteen to twenty vertical black bars on each side. Female usually only has two or three dark horizontal bars. Measures up to seven inches.

Distribution. Bays, estuaries, and coastal marshes.

Remarks. Small tidal marsh fish, they are the major prey of wading birds and fish-eating ducks and are also used as bait fish. They generally feed at the surface, using their upturned mouths to consume mosquito larvae and other insects.

MUMMICHOG (*Fundulus heteroclitus*)

Description. Blunt head and convex upper profile. Dark and silvery bars on sides, more in female than in the male. Measures up to five inches.

Distribution. Found principally in saltwater marshes and tidal creeks. Limited in fresh water.

Remarks. Small, hardy fish that can survive in extreme temperatures and low oxygen levels. Bait fish. Important in food chain because of distribution and abundance. Tolerant of stress and pollution.

ATLANTIC SEAHORSE (*Hippocampus hudsonus*)

Description. Highly variable color with large, pale blotches and dark lines lengthwise along back and neck. Measures up to six inches.

Distribution. Estuarine eelgrass and seaweed beds.

Atlantic seahorse

Remarks. Fairly common. Has a prehensile tail and a head resembling that of a horse. An unusual species, it is the male who "gives birth" to live young after the eggs are passed along by the female to his special broad pouch.

STRIPED BASS *(Morone saxatilis)*

Description. Silvery, with seven or eight black stripes on side; central stripes are the longest. The back is more olive in inshore waters and more blue offshore. Measures up to six feet and weighs up to 125 pounds.

Distribution. Coastal except to spawn.

Regulation. Minimum of thirty-eight inches.

Remarks. Important as food and game fish. Often caught with lures and live bait. Commercially fished with haul seines off Long Island. Found in Jamaica Bay during summer and fall. These are anadromous fish, spawning in fresh water and living in salt water.

BLUEFISH (*Pomatomus saltatrix*)

Description. Bluish or greenish on top. Silvery sides. Lateral line is nearly straight. Large mouth. Teeth are prominent, flattened, and triangular. Measures up to forty-five inches and weighs up to twenty-seven pounds.

Distribution. Tropical to temperate coasts; migrates to warmer waters. Follows small fish into shallow waters.

Regulation. Any size. Daily limit of ten fish.

Remarks. A popular sport fish, bluefish is aggressive and puts up a good fight when taken on a line. Known as snappers when young. Commonly taken with lures and bait.

A catch of striped bass, bluefish, and weakfish

SUMMER FLOUNDER OR FLUKE (*Paralichthys dentatus*)

Description. Compressed, with both eyes on left side. Large, toothy mouth. Measures up to thirty-seven inches and weighs up to twenty-six pounds.

Distribution. Bottom, warm-water fish preferring sand or mud.

Regulation. Minimum of fourteen inches.

Remarks. Can be caught using live bait such as killifish, squid pieces, jigs, small spoons, and spinners. Not a strong fighter, but provides lively action when taken on light tackle, unlike its less aggressive cousin, the winter flounder.

WINTER FLOUNDER (*Pleuronectes americanus*)

Description. Color and pattern vary. Straight lateral line. Small mouth. Area between the eyes is scaled. Measures up to twenty-five inches and weighs up to eight pounds. Compressed, with both eyes on right side.

Distribution. Like most bottom types, migrates to deep water in summer and shoals in winter. Found from November through June in Jamaica Bay.

Regulation. Minimum of ten inches.

Remarks. Jamaica Bay is a nursery for this species, which spends its first three years in the bay. A bottom feeder fond of the abundant populations of benthic amphipods found throughout Jamaica Bay.

ALEWIFE (*Alosa pseudoharengus*)

Description. Silvery with a greenish back and usually one small, dark shoulder spot with a large eye.

Distribution. Spawns in rivers.

Remarks. Commercially important.

BAY ANCHOVY (*Anchoa mitchilli*)

Description. Grayish, deep body. Has narrow, silvery stripe that is often faint or absent toward the front and fades after death. Short head. Very short snout with slightly overhanging mouth useful for plankton feeding. Measures up to four inches.

Distribution. Mostly shallow bays and estuaries.

Remarks. Anchovies tend to swim in dense schools with other bait fish. They are popular forage for bluefish and striped bass.

BLACKFISH (*Tautoga onitis*)

Description. Blunt snout. White chin. Males are dark olive to dark gray. White blotch on side. Females and young are mottled and blotched with darker gray to black on a paler olive to brownish background. Measures up to three feet and weighs up to twenty-two pounds.

Distribution. Coastal. Prefers pilings, breakwaters, and wrecks.

Regulation. Seven inches minimum in New Jersey.

Remarks. Young of the year are bright green, which serves as camouflage when they hide in the sea lettuce.

SCUP (*Stenotomus chrysops*)

Description. A dull silver with faint, irregular, dark bars on body and some pale blue flecks.

Distribution. Common in bays and shallow coastal waters.

Remarks. Popular sport fish of tropical coastal waters.

Reptiles and Amphibians

Of all the wild things at Gateway, amphibians and reptiles are the least popular with visitors. This could be because these species are harder to find than birds or plants, but many people have negative feelings about these animals—thinking of venomous snakes, snapping turtles, and poisonous frogs, for example.

I find these creatures fascinating, however, and at Gateway we are working to reintroduce extirpated snakes, turtles, frogs, and salamanders throughout the park. These species are important to our Hudson-Raritan estuary as food resources and for general biodiversity. We still have much to learn about these populations, though, and are annually monitoring these species throughout the park. Through a cooperative agreement with the Wildlife Conservation Society, formally the New York Zoological Society at the Bronx Zoological Park, for the past ten years Gateway has been breeding snake and amphibian species in captivity, releasing them into the Gateway wilds, and monitoring their progress. We are finding that by protecting habitat and sometimes manipulating surroundings (placing sticks in a pile as a hiding place, for example), we can help amphibians and reptiles to make a comeback.

Turtles

There are approximately fifty species of turtles in Canada and the United States. Found mostly near water, they have been negatively impacted by water pollutants.

The turtle is covered with hard shields known as scutes. The upper part of the shell is the carapace. The lower part, the plastron, in most cases indicates the sex, age, and species of the turtle.

SNAPPING TURTLE (*Chelydra serpentina*)

Description. Massive head and powerful jaws. Tan to dark brown shell. Distinctive ridged tail as long as shell. Underside is yellow to tan, unpatterned, and relatively small. Measures eight to twelve inches.

Distribution. Found throughout Gateway, primarily in freshwater ponds and streams.

Remarks. An omnivorous scavenger, it feeds on plant matter and carrion, and generally remains submerged. Seen most often in June, when females travel on land to lay eggs. Snapping turtles are aggressive and should be treated with extreme care.

BOX TURTLE (*Terrapene carolina*)

Description. Shell has high dome with ridges. Color varies from tan to dark brown, yellow, orange, or olive. Males usually have red eyes and depression in rear of plastron; females have yellowish brown eyes. Measures four to six and one-half inches.

Box turtle

Distribution. Terrestrial; found in uplands, woods, and shrub thickets. At Gateway they occur at Sandy Hook, Floyd Bennett Field, and Jamaica Bay Wildlife Refuge.

Remarks. Habitat loss and collection as pets has caused a great decline in regional box turtle populations. Locally collected animals have been released into the protected habitats at Gateway in an attempt to establish new populations.

DIAMONDBACK TERRAPIN (*Malaclemys terrapin*)

Description. Plastron is oblong with no hinge, and can be yellowish or greenish. Head and neck are gray and peppered with black. Light-colored jaws. Black, prominent eyes. Males are four to five and a half inches and females are six to nine and three-quarters inches.

Distribution. A salt marsh species that occurs throughout Gateway, primarily in shallow tidal creeks and flats.

Remarks. Females can be seen in early summer when they leave the marsh to nest in sandy areas. Disturbed soil along a trail may be a sign of a new nest. These turtles are of "critical concern" in New York State.

EASTERN PAINTED TURTLE (*Chrysemys picta*)

Description. Underside yellow, not patterned. Shell is olive or black; oval, smooth, and flattened; and has red bars or crescents on outer edges. Measures four to seven and seven-eighths inches.

Distribution. A widespread aquatic species found in ponds and wetlands throughout Gateway. Populations at Jamaica Bay Wildlife Refuge and Floyd Bennett Field were established by the National Park Service.

Remarks. Usually seen basking on logs and rocks. Feeds on aquatic vegetation and invertebrates.

RED-EARED SLIDER (*Chrysemys scripta elegans*)

Description. Red stripe behind eye. Oval shell is olive to brown in color. Chin is rounded. V-shaped notch at front of upper jaw. Measures five to eleven and three-eighths inches.

Distribution. Occasionally encountered in Gateway.

Remarks. This exotic species, a common pet, is not reproducing in Gateway.

ATLANTIC LOGGERHEAD (*Caretta caretta*)

Description. Has elongated, heart-shaped carapace with paddlelike limbs. This is the mostly commonly seen of the five sea species. Measures thirty-one to forty-eight inches.

Distribution. Ocean dwelling.

Remarks. Travels up the coast in late summer, feeding on marine invertebrates. Sometimes ingests plastic bags it mistakes for jellyfish.

Snakes

Snakes can be found in brush piles, under rocks and old wood, and near ponds and lakes. Look for their cast-off skins; they molt several times a year. Use extreme caution in areas of the park where snakes may be, because, although none are poisonous, they may bite when handled.

EASTERN HOGNOSE SNAKE (*Heteredon platyrhinos*)

Description. Stout body with pointed, upturned snout and wide neck. Variable color. Underside of the tail is conspicuously lighter than the belly. Measures twenty to forty-five and one-half inches.

Distribution. Typically found in sand dune habitats, this snake was once common on Sandy Hook and around Jamaica Bay, but habitat loss and pesticides are the probable causes of its declines. Attempts to restore populations at Breezy Point and Sandy Hook appear successful.

Remarks. These snakes have been known to play dead when threatened, and they give an excellent performance. They feed almost exclusively on Fowler's toad.

BLACK RACER (*Coluber constrictor*)

Description. Large, slender, agile, and fast moving. Adults are uniformly black, blue, brown, or greenish on top; white, yellow, or dark gray underneath. Measures thirty-four to seventy-seven inches.

Distribution. Found primarily in grassy, herbaceous habitats of the Jamaica Bay unit.

Remarks. Large, omnivorous snake uses speed to escape and will bite if threatened. Most frequently seen in spring and fall, basking on roads and trails.

MILK SNAKE *(Lampropeltis triangulum)*

Description. Gray or tan with a light Y-shaped or V-shaped patch on neck. Dark brown to reddish brown or black bordered blotches down back and sides. Can be colorfully ringed and blotched with orange-red, black, or white-yellow. Measures twelve to seventy-eight and one-quarter inches.

Distribution. Common along northern shore of Jamaica Bay; milk snakes at Gateway are limited to the Jamaica Bay unit.

Remarks. More than sixty milk snakes were released from 1984 to 1989, resulting in an established population in Jamaica Bay Wildlife Refuge. These snakes feed on rodents, birds, and other snakes.

BROWN SNAKE *(Storereia dekayi)*

Description. Small, gray, yellowish brown, brown, or reddish brown with two parallel rows of small dark spots bordering an indistinct, wide, light back stripe. Belly can be pale yellow, brown, or pinkish with small black dots along edges. This species gives birth to live young. Measures ten to twenty and three-quarters inches.

Distribution. Most commonly found in grassy and herbaceous habitats; occurs throughout Gateway.

Remarks. This small, secretive snake can survive some urbanization because of its small size and space requirements. Most Gateway populations are naturally occurring. Those at Jamaica Bay Wildlife Refuge, Floyd Bennett Field, and Fort Tilden are the result of restoration efforts. Feeds on worms and slugs.

COMMON GARTER SNAKE *(Thamnophis sirtalis)*

Description. Coloration is highly variable; back and side stripes are usually well defined. Side stripe is confined to second and third scale rows. Gives birth to live young. Measures eighteen to fifty-one and five-eighths inches.

Brown snakes

Distribution. Moist, grassy areas throughout Jamaica Bay unit and Great Kills.

Remarks. Diet includes insects, worms, small birds, and mammals.

Salamanders

Salamander populations are declining everywhere and the reasons are not clear. Pollution and habitat loss have taken their toll. Search for them near rotting logs and along wet areas.

SPOTTED SALAMANDER (*Ambystoma maculatum*)

Description. Stoutly built. Black, blue-black, dark gray, or dark brown on top with two irregular rows of round, yellow or orange spots from head to tail tip. Slate gray belly. Measures six to nine and three-quarters inches.

Distribution. Typically found in deciduous forest. Occurs at Jamaica Bay Wildlife Refuge as a result of restoration efforts.

Remarks. Burrowing salamander that emerges in early spring to migrate to breeding ponds.

REDBACK SALAMANDER (*Plethodon cinereus*)

Description. Long and slender with broad, straight-edged, dark-bordered stripe extending along back from head to tail. Stripe may be yellow, orange, pink, or gray. Belly has black-and-white mottling. Measures two and one-half to five inches.

Distribution. Found in leaf litter and logs. Occurs naturally in woodlands of Great Kills and has been introduced into the Jamaica Bay unit.

Remarks. Lungless, terrestrial species; lays eggs in rotting logs.

Frogs and Toads

Frogs and toads are nocturnal; they are difficult to observe during the day. Watch for them, though, near the pond areas on Floyd Bennett Field and Sandy Hook and at the marshes throughout the park.

SPADEFOOT TOAD (*Scaphiopus holbrooki*)

Description. Stout. Sickle-shaped spade on each hind foot is used for burrowing. External eardrum is apparent. Olive to brown to nearly black. Often has two irregular light lines down its back. Underside is white to grayish. Measures one and three-quarters to three and one-quarter inches.

Distribution. Forested, bushy, or cultivated areas of sandy, loose, or gravelly loam. At Gateway, only at Jamaica Bay Wildlife Refuge.

Remarks. Only breeds in years when there is excessive rainfall. Six hundred tadpoles were released at Big John's Pond in 1989; although some have survived to adulthood, the secretive nature of spadefoots makes population monitoring difficult.

FOWLER'S TOAD (*Bufo woodhousei fowleri*)

Description. Large toad with light stripe down middle of back. Prominent cranial crests. Color varies from yellow to green to brown. Measures two and one-half to five inches.

Distribution. Occurs in dry, sandy areas throughout Gateway. Breeds in small ponds in spring. Shady Hook's North Pond is a great place to listen for them from late April through May.

Spadefoot toad

Remarks. Fowler's toad is the common toad of the Northeast coast. Because its requirements are fairly simple, it is one of few amphibian species capable of surviving in urban areas.

SPRING PEEPER (*Hyla crucifer*)

Description. Tan, brown, or gray with characteristic dark X on back; large toe pads. Measures three-quarters to one and three-eighths inches.

Distribution. Wooded areas in or near permanent or temporarily flooded ponds and swamps. Occurs at Staten Island and Jamaica Bay units.

Remarks. Adults are terrestrial. Eggs are laid in ponds in early spring. Choruses can be heard from late March through April at Big John's Pond at the Jamaica Bay Wildlife Refuge and at the Return-a-Gift Pond at Floyd Bennett Field.

Spring peeper

Gray treefrog

GRAY TREEFROG (*Hyla versicolor*)

Description. Rough skin. Greenish, brownish, or gray with several large dark blotches on back. Dark-edged light spot beneath eye. Underside of thigh is bright yellow-orange. Has large toe pads. Measures one and one-quarter to two and three-eighths inches.

Distribution. Found at Gateway at Jamaica Bay Wildlife Refuge and Floyd Bennett Field as a result of population restoration.

Remarks. Terrestrial arboreal species that lays eggs in pond. Males can be heard calling in May and June at Big John's and Return-a-Gift Ponds.

GREEN FROG (*Rana clamitans melanota*)

Description. Green, bronze, or brown. Has large external eardrum. Green upper lip. White belly with darker pattern of lines or spots. Male has yellow throat and swollen thumb. Measures two and one-eighth to four inches.

Distribution. The green frog is the most aquatic amphibian at Gateway and feeds along pond edges. Hibernates in muddy bottom. Occurs along Duck and Mill Creeks, at Great Kills, and has been released into Big John's Pond.

Remarks. Males heard in May and June; call sounds like a loose-stringed banjo. Tadpoles become frogs in two years.

BIRDS

Gateway lies on the Atlantic flyway, the main migratory route for birds along the Atlantic coastline. Each spring and fall this highway in the sky is traveled by millions of birds. Because of Gateway's position on the flyway, visitors can observe more than 340 bird species there during the span of a year.

Along the shoreline of Breezy Point and Sandy Hook you can see oystercatchers; common, least, and roseate terns; and a host of other coastal birds. From late March through September the National Park Service protects one of the most concentrated colonies of one endangered species, piping plover. The plovers share their habitat at Breezy Point with two of their competitors, great black-backed and herring gulls. Pyrotechnics are used to scare the adult gulls away, and exclosures (wire mesh nets) are used to prevent the gulls and other predators from preying on plover chicks or eggs. Another endangered species that is a common visitor during its immature stage of development is the American bald eagle.

Since Gateway is open year-round, winter birds can be seen along trails throughout the park. If you are truly a beachcomber you'll see plenty of dunlins.

Human influence on the survival of migrant species has been dramatic. Habitat manipulation designed to support birds that have been extirpated because of accumulation of foreign chemicals (xenobiotics) in the environment or habitat loss has helped several species rebound from the brink of extinction. Placing osprey poles in the estuary, for example, has encouraged this bird to nest in Jamaica Bay, and in 1994 there were two nesting pairs in the refuge. Several pairs at the Sandy Hook unit were also nesting and breeding.

Even if we cannot provide habitat by restoring the natural landscape, the man-made environment around the park (bridges, buildings, and so on) can act as habitat. Peregrine falcons, for example, are making a come-back from DDT-decimated population levels; these falcons are now thriving, with nine nesting pairs in the New York City area in 1993 and other nests on the Marine Parkway bridge over the Rockaway Inlet to Jamaica Bay. The bridge has been designated a critical habitat by the New York State Department of Environmental Conservation (NYSDEC).

HORNED GREBE (Podiceps auritus)

Description. Dark back. Rufous neck, breast, and flank. White belly. Short, straight bill. Brilliant red eyes. Golden ear tufts above the eyes. Measures twelve to fifteen inches. Black or gray; white in winter (non-breeding plumage).

Distribution. Found during breeding season on interior freshwater marshes, ponds, and slow-moving rivers. Winters on coastal saltwater and nearby lakes.

Remarks. Common winter resident in Jamaica Bay. They feed on small fish, frogs, snails, and insects. As do other grebes, they regularly eat feathers. Ornithologists believe the feathers help strain out undigestible bits of shell or bone.

RED-THROATED LOON (Gavia stellata)

Description. Red throat patch. Black-and-white stripes on nape. Pale gray head. Slender, uptilted bill. Winter plumage gray above, white below. Measures up to twenty-five inches.

Distribution. Found along shorelines with shallow water and in estuaries.

Remarks. Uncommon in winter. Extremely vulnerable to oil pollution; many have died in oil spills.

COMMON LOON (Gavia immer)

Description. Heavy, black bill. Black head. White necklace. Densely checkered back with small spots.

Distribution. Protected bays, estuaries, and lakes.

Remarks. Uncommon winter resident. Occasionally summers in bays. Eats mainly fish. Known for its bucolic call.

DOUBLE-CRESTED CORMORANT (*Phalacrocorax auritus*)

Description. Adults are black with iridescent green and purple on upper parts. Yellow or orange unfeathered throat pouch. Black bill and feet. Blue-green iris. Flies with distinctive crooked neck. Measures twenty-six to thirty-two inches.

Distribution. Easily adapts to marine and freshwater areas along entire coastline of park.

Remarks. Cormorants perch on old pilings, rock outcroppings, flagpoles, or light poles near the shore. The Japanese use cormorants to hunt fish. They tie a noose around the bird's neck so that it can't swallow the fish and let it dive for prey. When a bird catches a fish, it is brought back into the boat and the fish is removed from the cormorant's throat. This bird spreads its wings to dry; it doesn't preen its wings from an oil gland, as other aquatic birds do.

GREAT EGRET (*Casmerodius albus*)

Description. White with a yellow bill. Black legs and feet. Long white plumes on back. Measures thirty-seven to forty-one inches.

Distribution. Most common heron. Found in freshwater and salt-water marshes and lagoons, lakes, and ponds.

Remarks. Common nesting species. Feeds on fish, frogs, snakes, and crayfish. Once hunted for its plumes, it is protected and is the national emblem of the National Audubon Society.

SNOWY EGRET (*Egretta thula*)

Description. Small, slender, and white. Slender, black bill. Yellow, unfeathered lores—has longer plumes on head, back, and breast during breeding season. Black legs and yellow feet. Measures twenty-two to twenty-six inches.

Distribution. Most wetland habitats of Gateway.

Remarks. Slaughtered in nineteenth and early twentieth centuries for their fine white plumes, which were used to decorate women's hats. It breeds within park boundaries.

Great egret

BLACK-CROWNED NIGHT HERON (*Nycticorax nycticorax*)

Description. Small and stocky with short bill, neck, and legs. Black cap and back. Gray wings. Measures twenty-three to twenty-six inches.

Distribution. Marshes, wooded swamps, and forests along rivers and streams. Can frequently be seen along pond edges at the Jamaica Bay Wildlife Refuge.

Remarks. Nocturnal; spends the day roosting in trees or reeds. Breeds in the park.

GLOSSY IBIS (*Plegadis falcinellus*)

Description. Dark, heronlike wading bird with a long, down-curved bill. Adults in spring and summer are colorful, with a rich chestnut neck and breast with purple gloss on head, neck, underparts, and shoulders. Lower back wings and tail are more greenish or brassy. Measures nineteen to twenty-six inches.

Glossy ibis

Distribution. Marshes and estuaries. For most of the century, this bird was confined to Florida and the Gulf states; it has extended its range.

Remarks. Common summer nester. Eats insects and snakes; probes for mollusks in the mud with its downward-curved bill. Breeds in the park.

AMERICAN BITTERN (*Botaurus lentiginosus*)

Description. Brown, streaked plumage. Black neck stripe. Dull green legs. Up to twenty-eight inches in length.

Distribution. Fresh or brackish marshes, especially among cattails and rushes.

Remarks. Regular migrant and winter resident of park. Sensitive and relies on its coloring for protection. Often "freezes," with neck and bill pointed upward when alarmed.

LEAST BITTERN (*Ixobrychus exilis*)

Description. Large, pale buff wing patches and rich, dark chestnut on rest of wings and sides of neck. Dull, green legs. Pale bill. Up to thirteen inches.

Distribution. Prefers freshwater marshes but occasionally breeds in brackish areas.

Remarks. Rare nesting species in freshwater ponds.

MUTE SWAN (*Cygnus olor*)

Description. White with pink bill that becomes orange-red in breeding season. Hazel eyes. Black legs and feet. Measures fifty to sixty inches.

Distribution. Year-round resident in ponds, rivers, and coastal bays. Most widespread swan in North America; introduced from Europe in nineteenth century.

Remarks. Flocks fly in V formations. Can be very aggressive, especially in defense of a nest. Considered exotic. Breeds in refuge.

CANADA GOOSE (*Branta canadensis*)

Description. Black bill, legs, and feet. Black head and neck with white cheek patch. White belly. Measures twenty-two to twenty-seven inches.

Distribution. Grassy areas throughout the park.

Remarks. They are among the fastest flying geese and are popular game birds. Breeds in the park.

BRANT *(Branta bernicla)*

Description. Dark belly. Short, black neck. White neck collar. White undertail. Short, stubby, black bill. Black legs. Measures twenty-two to twenty-six inches.

Distribution. Coastal bays.

Remarks. Common in winter. Gateway is at the northern extreme of its nesting range.

BLACK DUCK *(Anas rubripes)*

Description. Sooty brown body. Pale head and neck. Purple speculum, or quill feathers.

Distribution. Marshes and estuaries.

Remarks. Common year-round resident. Game bird.

MALLARD *(Anas platyrhynchos)*

Description. Female is uniformly mottled with dull orange-and-brown bill and whitish tail feathers; dark blue speculum with white borders. Male has a green head, chestnut breast, and blue speculum.

Distribution. Lakes, marshes, and swamps.

Remarks. Common year-round. Strong flier. Ancestor of domestic white duck.

BLUE-WINGED TEAL *(Anas discors)*

Description. Female has gray-brown plumage, pale spot on lores, and distinct dark line through the eye. Male has bluish gray head with white crescent on face, and white flank patch; blue-gray wing coverts are visible in flight.

Distribution. Grassy areas and shallow marshes.

Remarks. Uncommon migrant and wintering species. Breeds in the park.

GREEN-WINGED TEAL (Anas crecca)

Description. Rust-colored head, green face with vertical eye patch. White stripe on side. Females are gray-brown with a dark eyeline and buff triangular patch on dark undertail. Measures twelve to sixteen inches.

Distribution. Mudflats, shallow marshes, and lake borders. Observed throughout the park.

Remarks. Favorite winter food is eelgrass. Call of female is a soft quack; the male whistles.

AMERICAN WIGEON (Anas americana)

Description. Medium-sized. Round, green head. Narrow wings. Short, pale blue bill with a black tip. Wedge-shaped tail. Breeding males have a white crown on the head. White wing patch visible in flight. Measures eighteen to twenty-three inches.

Distribution. Ponds and marshes.

Remarks. Uncommon winter resident. Can be seen on marshy ponds with diving birds but is a dabbling duck.

BUFFLEHEAD (Bucephala albeola)

Description. Large head, small body. Adult male has a black back, white sides, iridescent purple neck, and an iridescent green head with a large white patch behind the eye. Female has a dark brown head and body and white cheeks. Smallest North American waterfowl. Measures thirteen to fifteen and one-half inches.

Distribution. Bays, harbors, and ice-free lakes in winter. Also found at the Sandy Hook unit.

Remarks. Common in winter. Breeds in trees. Look for male breeding displays throughout winter: it bobs its head and flaps it wings.

CANVASBACK (Aythya valisineria)

Description. Female has sandy brown head and neck, grayish back. Male has chestnut head and neck; white back, sides, and inner wing; black breast; red eye. Both have broadly sloping foreheads and long, black bills.

Distribution. Inland lakes and coastal bays.

Remarks. Uncommon winter resident. Usually found with scaup.

GREATER SCAUP (Aythya marila)

Description. Male has rounded head, black chest and rump, and gray back. Female has rounded, brown head with large, white patch at the base of the bill; dark brown back; gray-brown flanks. Both have pale blue bills.

Distribution. Open marine environments, bays, and estuaries.

Remarks. Large flocks winter in Jamaica and Sandy Hook Bays.

LESSER SCAUP (Aythya affinis)

Description. Female has peaked, brown head with small white patch at the base of the bill, dark brown back, and gray-brown flanks. Male has peaked head, black chest and rump, pale gray back, and short, white wing stripe. Both have pale blue bills with dark tips.

Distribution. Small ponds and marshes, protected harbors, and brackish bays.

Remarks. Uncommon, but sometimes there are large flocks on ponds at refuge; winter resident.

RUDDY DUCK (Oxyura jamaicensis)

Description. Small and chunky with small neck. Breeding male has blue bill, white cheeks, black head, rufous body, and long tail. In non-breeding season it has brown cap, mottled cheeks, and long tail. Female is brown with dark slash across cheek, blue bill. Measures fifteen to sixteen inches.

Distribution. Marshy lakes and ponds.

Remarks. Uncommon year-round resident. Seldom flies. Uses marsh vegetation as camouflage to protect nest. Eggs are huge for such a small duck. Breeds in the park.

GADWALL (Anas strepera)

Description. Distinctive characteristic is the white underside of its secondary feathers. Male has a gray body, sandy brown head, and black undertail. Female has narrow gray bill with orange edge, and is uniformly mottled brown. Measures eighteen to twenty-two and one-half inches.

Distribution. Freshwater marshes, ponds, and rivers and Gateway salt marshes in the Jamaica Bay Wildlife Refuge.

Remarks. A popular game bird that is very abundant in southern United States marshes in winter. Breeds in the park.

WHITE-WINGED SCOTER (*Melanitta fusca*)

Description. Short-necked, heavy-headed bird. Male has reddish orange bill with black knob at the base, small white mark behind eye, and white speculum. Female has long bill, pale spots on sides of dark head, and dark brown body.

Distribution. Common along Atlantic coast in winter.

Remarks. Feeds on clams, mussels, and other mollusks. Very rare in Jamaica Bay Wildlife Refuge.

OLD-SQUAW (*Clangula hyemalis*)

Description. Female has short bill and dark upper parts. Male has bold black-and-white back pattern; long, thin, black tail feathers; and dark wings. Both have white heads with dark patches.

Distribution. Breeds on arctic tundra but observed along both Atlantic and Pacific coasts during the winter.

Remarks. Uncommon winter resident. Most often found near bay mouths.

COMMON GOLDENEYE (*Bucephala clangula*)

Description. Female has a brown head, grayish back and sides, and dark bill with small, yellowish patch. Male has white sides, black back, and glossy green head with white spot at the base of the bill.

Distribution. Large lakes, impoundments, and rivers.

Remarks. Regular winter resident. Also called whistler for sound produced by wings.

SEMIPALMATED PLOVER (*Charadrius melodus*)

Description. Stubby bill. Tip of bill is black, the rest orange. Legs are orange. Brown upper parts, white forehead with black bar across top of head, black ring around neck, white breast. Measures six and one-half to seven and one-half inches.

Distribution. Mudflats, beaches, and plowed fields.

Remarks. Common during migration. Migrate in flocks but scatter when feeding. The word *semipalmated* means half-webbed; the birds' toes are partially webbed about half their length.

BLACK-BELLIED PLOVER (*Pluvialis squatarola*)

Description. Large plover with short, stubby bill. Black face and breast. Whitish cap. Mottled body. Black legs. Summer plumage is black belly with a grayish, speckled back. Black "underarms" during winter lend bird its name. Measures ten and one-half to thirteen and one-half inches.

Distribution. Salt marshes, tidal flats, and seacoasts.

Remarks. Common during migration. Largest plover, usually flies alone. Winters in the park.

GREATER YELLOWLEGS (*Tringa melanolevca*)

Description. Long, yellow legs. Long, slightly upturned bill. Dark upper parts. Streak and bars on breast and belly. Measures twelve and one-half to fifteen inches.

Distribution. Shallow ponds, lakes, tidal creeks, and marshes.

Remarks. Common during migration. Noisy and conspicuous. Feeds in tide pools.

WILLET (*Catoptrophorus semipalmatus*)

Description. Long, heavy, straight bill. White rump. Drab, gray-brown plumage. Blue-gray legs. Measures fourteen to sixteen and one-quarter inches.

Distribution. Coastal marshes and nearby grassy areas. Found throughout Gateway.

Remarks. Common marsh-nesting species. Noisy "willet" call. The willet is a shorebird; however, it often perches on trees, bushes, and fences. When landing, it holds its dramatically marked wings over its head.

RUDDY TURNSTONE (*Arenaria interpres*)

Description. Stout, wedge-shaped bill. Black and white head. Rusty back. Black bib. White belly. Orange-red legs. Measures seven and three-quarters to nine and one-quarter inches.

Distribution. Coastal rocks and jetties and sandy beaches.

Remarks. Common migrant. A few overwinter in the Jamaica Bay Wildlife Refuge.

PIPING PLOVER (*Charadrius melodus*)

Description. Bright orange legs. Narrow black breastband. Black headband. Short, stubby bill with orange base. White rump. Measures six to eight inches.

Piping plover

Distribution. Nests in colonies at the Breezy Point Tip area and Sandy Hook.

Remarks. Threatened species of waterbirds. Gateway has a nationally significant and important colony at Breezy Point and Sandy Hook. The chicks are preyed on by a host of predators, but human disturbance is the major problem. The number of birds fledged in the park has tripled since 1988.

KILLDEER *(Charadrius vociferus)*

Description. Two black bands on breast. Long tail. Long, flesh-colored legs. Brown upper parts. Bright red eye ring. Thin, black bill.

Distribution. Lawns, pastures, plowed fields, prairies, mudflats, and shorelines. Observed throughout the park.

Remarks. Nests just above high-tide areas. Song sounds like its name. One of the first shorebirds to arrive in spring and one of the last to leave in fall. Will fake a broken wing to distract potential predator away from young.

AMERICAN OYSTERCATCHER *(Haematopus palliatus)*

Description. Prominent red bill. Yellow eyes with red rims. Orange legs. White breast. Black head and neck. Measures seventeen to twenty-one inches.

Distribution. Barrier islands and coastal marshes. Sandy, rocky shores and rocky, intertidal areas.

Remarks. Common summer nesting species. Uses its bladelike bill to open bivalves.

LESSER YELLOWLEGS *(Tringa flavipes)*

Description. Long, yellow legs. Thin, straight, black bill. Streaked breast. White rump.

Distribution. Ponds, lakeshores, tidal mudflats; marsh and tundra in breeding season.

Remarks. Common migrant. Occurs in large flocks.

SEMIPALMATED SANDPIPER *(Calidris pusilla)*

Description. In winter has dark legs, whitish eyebrow, grayish brown upper parts. During breeding season its plumage is grayish brown and black on its upper parts with light rufous edges. Band of streaks across upper breast. Measures five and one-half to seven inches.
Distribution. Tidal flats, lagoons, and ponds.
Remarks. Probably the most common North American shorebird at Gateway; occurs in huge flocks.

SPOTTED SANDPIPER *(Actitis macularia)*

Description. Gray-brown upper parts. White wing stripe. In springtime, prominent spotted underparts. Pink and black bill. Black line through eye. Length is seven to eight inches.
Distribution. Seacoasts, inland lakes, and rivers. Summer resident from mid-April to October.
Remarks. Common migrant. Nicknames like "tip-up" or "teeter-tail" point out the characteristic by which this bird can be identified: continuously tipping forward and backward. Breeds in the park.

SANDERLING *(Calidris alba)*

Description. Conspicuous, white wing stripe. White rump divided by a broad, black median line. Black legs and feet. Straight, black, slightly tapered bill. Length is seven to eight inches.
Distribution. Tidal flats, lake beaches, and sandbars. Found on beaches in winter, especially Riis Park and Sandy Hook beaches.
Remarks. Common migrant. Feeds right at the edge of the water, where incoming waves drop their loads of food. A line of birds will scamper forward, eating on the run, then retreat as the next wave approaches.

DUNLIN *(Calidris alpina)*

Description. Gray winter plumage. Rusty upper parts, and black belly during breeding season. Drooped bill. Black legs. Black patch on belly.
Distribution. Coastal tidal flats, lagoons, beaches, and mudflats. Usually found on mudflats in bays or along the beaches of the Atlantic

during winter. Large numbers seen along ocean beaches at Riis Park and Sandy Hook.

Remarks. Common winter species. Feeds on marine worms. Winters in the park.

RED KNOT (*Calidris canutus*)

Description. Rufous face and underparts. Dark brown upper parts with white and rufous feather edges. Straight, black, slightly tapered bill. Dark legs and feet. Breeding adult has rufous-chestnut underparts and face with white on the lower belly through to the undertail. Winter plumage is medium gray. Measures ten to eleven inches.

Distribution. Coastal beaches and salt marshes.

Remarks. Common migrant. Feeds in great numbers on horseshoe crab eggs in May and June.

LEAST SANDPIPER (*Calidris minutilla*)

Description. Slightly drooped, black bill. Sooty brown upper parts with narrow chestnut and buff edges. Yellowish legs and feet. Measures five to six and one-half inches.

Distribution. Wet, muddy, or grassy areas, salt marshes, and tidal flats.

Remarks. The smallest sandpiper.

SHORT-BILLED DOWITCHER (*Limnodromus griseus*)

Description. Medium-sized shorebird with chunky body. Very long, straight, heavy bill. Wedge of white up the rump and back. Barred tail.

Distribution. Shallow ponds, open marshes, salt or brackish water. Greatest numbers in May and July to October.

Remarks. Common migrant. Occurs in large flocks. Feeding habit often described like a sewing machine, as bird repeatedly thrusts bill into soft mud as it walks to capture invertebrates.

AMERICAN WOODCOCK (*Scolopax minor*)

Description. Very long bill. Barred crown. Rust-colored underparts. Large, dark, high-set eyes. Ten to twelve inches long. Chunky, short-legged.

Distribution. Found in moist thickets and woodlands.

Remarks. Although classified as a shorebird, it is rarely found at shorelines. Likes open, grassy patches, where it performs its spring courtship flights.

WILSON'S PHALAROPE (Phalaropus tricolor)

Description. Female has a fine, straight, black bill; pale crown and nape; dark stripe through eye and down neck. Male has a brown crown; brown and chestnut line from eye down neck; black legs. Both have chestnut breasts. Eight to ten inches in length.

Distribution. Freshwater and saltwater marshes, lakes, and coastal bays.

Remarks. Rare but regular migrant. Does not have fully lobed toes, so rarely swims. During breeding, it is the colorful females that do the courting and the drab males that build the nests, lay the eggs, and raise the young!

HERRING GULL (Larus argentatus)

Description. Yellow bill with orange spot. Distinctive yellow eye and eye ring. Pale gray body with white plumage. Pinkish legs. Measures twenty-three to twenty-six inches.

Distribution. Scavenger birds found at garbage dumps and beaches. Most abundant and widespread gull.

Remarks. Common year-round. A widespread species that plays an important role in cleaning up harbors and beaches as a scavenger. Well known for dropping shellfish on rocks and roads to crack them open.

LAUGHING GULL (Larus atricilla)

Description. Black head and wing tips. Red, drooping bill. White breast and rump. White eye crescents. Measures sixteen to seventeen inches. It gets its name from its "ha-ha-ha" call.

Distribution. Beaches and salt marshes.

Remarks. Laughing call. JoCo marsh and adjacent islands in Jamaica Bay have the only breeding colony in New York State.

RING-BILLED GULL (*Larus delawarensis*)

Description. Black band on yellow bill. Bright yellowish legs. Pale yellow eyes. Pale gray mantle. Measures eighteen to twenty inches.
Distribution. Mudflats, beaches, and wet fields.
Remarks. Winter visitor to the park.

BONAPARTE'S GULL (*Larus philadelphia*)

Description. Small, black bill. Black head. White eye crescent. Red legs. Small with neat, pointed wings and square tail. In winter, a white leading wing edge is distinctive. Length is twelve to fourteen inches.
Distribution. Bays, inlets, and coastal waters. Breeds in northern coniferous forests.
Remarks. Winter visitor. This gull is named after a nephew of Napoleon, Charles Lucien Bonaparte, a leading ornithologist in the 1800s in America and Europe.

GREAT BLACK-BACKED GULL (*Larus marinus*)

Description. Black body. Yellow bill with orange spot at tip. Pinkish legs. Measures twenty-eight to thirty-one inches.
Distribution. Colonies at Breezy Point.
Remarks. Largest gull found in Gateway. Year-round resident. Predator of seabirds.

COMMON TERN (*Sterna hirundo*)

Description. Red bill. Black cap. White breast and neck. Gray body. Measures thirteen to sixteen inches.
Distribution. Nests in colonies on beaches and in salt marshes. Seen nesting at Breezy Point and Sandy Hook.
Remarks. Nests are depressions in the sand that are sparsely lined with shells and pebbles. Dives for small fish. Its acrobatics along the shore are entertaining. Breeds in the park.

LEAST TERN (*Sterna antillarum*)

Description. Yellow bill with black tip. White forehead. Black cap. Yellow legs. Gray wings. White breast. Measures eight and one-half to nine and one-half inches.

Distribution. Found along coastal beaches. Winters in the tropics. Nests at Breezy Point.

Remarks. New York State endangered species. Smallest tern. Nicknamed "the little striker" for the way it plunges into the water for fish.

ROSEATE TERN (*Sterna dougalli*)

Description. Black bill and cap. White neck and breast. Gray upper body. Slender bill. Measures fourteen to sixteen inches.

Distribution. Islands and protected sand spits.

Remarks. Federally designated endangered species. One nesting pair was recorded at Breezy Point in 1993. Other species, such as the roseate tern, benefit from efforts to protect the coastal habitat for plovers.

BLACK SKIMMER (*Rynchops niger*)

Description. Red-and-black bill. Lower bill is longer than upper bill. Black head and upper body. White underside. Measures sixteen to twenty inches.

Distribution. Marine bays and ocean beaches. Found at Breezy Point.

Remarks. Glides over water, skimming fish with lower bill. Feeds mostly at night, when fish are near the surface.

SHARP-SHINNED HAWK (*Accipiter striatus*)

Description. Small, fast-flying hawk. Short, rounded wings and long, square-tipped tail, which is identifying characteristic. Ten to fourteen inches in length.

Distribution. Dense coniferous forests. Uncommon in the summer and rare in winter. Nests in trees.

Remarks. Preys on small birds, such as sparrows and warblers, as well as small rodents and insects.

Sharp-shinned hawk

Red-tailed hawk

COOPER'S HAWK (*Accipiter cooperii*)

Description. Long tail with short, rounded wings. Rounded tail tip.

Distribution. Deciduous and coniferous forests. Observed parkwide, especially at Jamaica Bay Wildife Refuge and Floyd Bennett Field.

Remarks. Long tail gives maneuverability when bird pursues prey.

RED-TAILED HAWK (*Buteo jamaicensis*)

Description. Larger than the common crow. Chestnut-red tail visible during soaring. Wingspan to four and one-half feet. Throat and underparts white.

Distribution. A regular yet uncommon winter resident; can be observed across woodland areas of the park.

Remarks. Highways and aircraft have taken their toll on these birds of prey. This hawk feeds on mice, other small rodents, and occasionally small birds. Breeds in the park.

AMERICAN KESTREL (*Falco sparverius*)

Description. About the size of a robin. Has beautiful pointed, long, colorful wings. Female has rufous underparts with black barring and a rufous banded tail. Male has bluish, pointed wings and a red tail with a dark band near tip. Both have two marks on cheek.

Distribution. Habitats include deserts, forest openings, marshes, grasslands, cities, and suburbs. Nests are generally in a natural cavity in a tree or an abandoned woodpecker hole.

Remarks. Feeds extensively on insects, yet may take mice, snakes, or frogs. The Park Service has released more than fifty rehabilitated kestrels on Floyd Bennett Field since 1987.

RING-NECKED PHEASANT (*Phasianus colchicus*)

Description. Female has mottled brown plumage and pointed tail with no white markings. Male has a glossy green head with a red face patch; white necklace and long tail.

Distribution. Fields, brush, and woods. Large numbers at Floyd Bennett Field and Great Kills.

Male and female ring-necked pheasant

Remarks. Common year-round resident. Considered exotic. Feeds on seeds, buds, and plant shoots. Early in the morning males will be close to roadways, and vehicles will startle them into the brush.

MOURNING DOVE (*Zenaida macroura*)

Description. Uniform, gray-brown color with slight iridescence along neck. Small head. Thin neck. Long, tapered tail with white feather tips.

Distribution. Everywhere but densely forested regions. Feeds on seed.

Remarks. Common year-round. Soft cooing is often mistaken for owl's hooting. Breeds in the park.

SHORT-EARED OWL (*Asio flammeus*)

Description. Long, wide wings with a mothlike flight. Dark wrist mark. Pale buff area at base of primaries. Small facial disk with yellow eyes surrounded by black feathers. Short, thick neck.

Distribution. Open areas, such as tundra, moorland, marshes, dunes, grasslands, and agricultural fields. Found in grasslands at Floyd Bennett Field, where most recent documented nesting in New York City occurred.

Remarks. Winter resident. Visible most evenings; hunts along grassland periphery. Bred in the park up to 1970s.

LONG-EARED OWL (*Asio otus*)

Description. Long ear tufts. Orange-chestnut facial discs. Vertical markings on belly. Measures thirteen to sixteen inches.

Distribution. Breeds from northern Canada; migrates to Virginia and farther south in winter. Observed throughout the park.

Remarks. Uncommon winter resident of pine groves. Very secretive and difficult to see.

SNOWY OWL (*Nyctea scandiaca*)

Description. White plumage with some dark bars or spots. No ear tufts. Measures twenty to twenty-seven inches.

Distribution. Has been observed throughout the park. Winter resident of open fields.

Remarks. Shows very little fear of humans or their activities. Is often seen along concrete runways on Floyd Bennett Field or at Breezy Point and the Jamaica Bay Wildlife Refuge ponds.

SAW-WHET OWL (*Aegolius acadicus*)

Description. Very small, yellow-eyed owl with no ear tufts.

Distribution. Evergreen thickets in parks and isolated pines.

Remarks. Preys on mice and other small rodents at night. Except for the pygmy owl, the saw-whet is the smallest owl along the east coast.

Saw-whet owl

BELTED KINGFISHER (*Ceryle torquata*)

Description. Large, small-footed, heavy-headed, long-billed bird with bushy crest, white collar, and blue-gray upper parts and chest band. Rufous lower breast and belly.

Distribution. Nests in dirt banks along rivers, lakes, and saltwater estuaries.

Remarks. Common migrant. May hover over water where fish are visible and dive directly down for prey. Loud chattering call.

CHIMNEY SWIFT (*Chaetura pelagica*)

Description. Uniform brown upper parts. Pale throat and upper breast. Stiff tail with projecting spikes. Four to five inches in length. Bow-shaped wings.

Distribution. Breeds and roosts in chimneys. Previously roosted in hollow trees.

Remarks. Common migrant. A fast flier, it feeds only on flying insects. In flight looks like a flying cigar. Wintering locations for chimney swifts were unknown until fairly recently, when it was discovered that the entire population migrates to remote parts of the upper Amazon.

DOWNY WOODPECKER (*Picoides pubescens*)

Description. Short bill. Male has red nape patch. Black bars on outer tail feathers. Unmarked white underparts. White eyebrow. Black eye stripe.

Distribution. Parks, orchards, gardens, forests, and woodlands.

Remarks. Common migrant and winter resident in park woodlands. Breeds in the park.

HORNED LARK (*Eremophila alpestris*)

Description. Stocky ground bird with pinkish brown back. Striped facial patterns. Black chest band. Black tail with white outer tail feathers. Yellow face. Has small, black feather tufts on forward crown.

Distribution. Open habitats.

Remarks. Nests at Breezy Point and elsewhere in the park. Feeds mainly on seeds, occasionally on various insects.

BLUE JAY (*Cyanocitta cristata*)

Description. Head has a prominent blue crest. Upper parts are blue with large white spots on wing and tail. Black necklace. Long, blue tail with white tips. Nine and one-half to twelve inches long.

Distribution. Common, especially where oak and pine forests predominate.

Remarks. Uncommon on Jamaica Bay; more common in wooded areas, such as Staten Island and Sandy Hook. Omnivorous, they feed on fruits, seeds, nuts, insects, birds' eggs, small birds, mice, snails, and even fish.

AMERICAN CROW (*Corvus brachyrhynchos*)

Description. Entirely black with slight purplish gloss. Square tail. Large bill. Black legs. Length is sixteen to twenty inches.

Distribution. Open and semiopen habitats.

Remarks. Common year-round. Frequently observed "mobbing" other larger birds of prey, such as hawks and owls.

BARN SWALLOW (*Hirundo rustica*)

Description. Only swallow with long, deeply forked tail with white spots. Blue-black upper parts. Rust underparts. Five and one-half to seven inches long.

Distribution. Nests on or near buildings, under bridges or wharves, on rocky ledges over streams, inside sheds, or in culverts.

Remarks. Common resident from mid-April to late September. Nests are made of mud mixed with dried grass and lined with fine grasses and feathers. Feeds almost entirely on insects while in flight. Breeds in the park.

TREE SWALLOW (*Tachycineta bicolor*)

Description. Dark green-blue underparts. Dark crown extending to eye. Notched tail. Wide-based, triangular wings. Swift, darting flight. Four and one-half to five and one-half inches long.

Distribution. Forages for insects near bodies of brackish water such as ponds, small lakes, marshes, and wet meadows. May overwinter at Gateway.

Remarks. Cavity nester. At Gateway, nests in boxes.

MARSH WREN (*Cistothorus palustris*)

Description. Bold, white eyebrow. Unstreaked crown. White stripes on back; lower back and scapulars are rust. Long, thin, curved bill. Tail is upright; occasionally flicks tail as it hunts the undergrowth.

Distribution. Inhabits marshes, pond shores, and tidal river banks.

Remarks. Breeds in Phragmites, reeds, and cattails.

NORTHERN MOCKINGBIRD (*Mimus polyglottos*)

Description. Slender, long-tailed, gray bird with white patches on wings and tail. Nine to eleven inches in length.

Distribution. Open field habitats, scrubby growth near water.

Remarks. Common year-round. Very territorial. Can imitate sounds of many different species of birds, frogs, crickets, or dogs.

BROWN THRASHER (*Toxostoma rufum*)

Description. Rufous crown, back, wings, and tail with two dull white wing bars. White underparts with dark brown streaks. Curved bill. Long tail. Nine and one-half to eleven inches long.

Distribution. Thickets and fields with scrub and woodland borders.

Remarks. Thicket nester. Feeds on ground. Breeds, but becoming rare and local.

WOOD THRUSH (*Hylocichla mustelina*)

Description. Brown upper parts. Bright, rusty head. White under-parts with large blackish spots.

Distribution. Moist, deciduous woodlands. Primarily a bird of the forest floor and understory.

Remarks. Common migrant. Can be observed from early May to late October. Most familiar spotted brown thrush. Nests around houses. Insects and fruit constitute most of its food.

HERMIT THRUSH (*Catharus guttatus*)

Description. Brown, spotted thrush with dull brown upper parts and rusty tail. Six to seven and one-half inches long.

Distribution. Forests, woodlands, and thickets.

Remarks. Common migrant. Only spotted thrush that winters in northern states.

MYRTLE WARBLER (*Dendroica coroneta*)

Description. Similar to yellow-rumped warbler, but has a white throat.

Distribution. Variable during migration and winter.

Remarks. Only warbler that regularly winters in the northern states, when its diet shifts from insects to bayberries.

YELLOW WARBLER (*Dendroica petechia*)

Description. Bright yellow with light, olive green tinge on back. Male has fine, rusty streaks on breast. Yellow spots on tail. Four to five inches in length.

Distribution. Moist thickets along streams and swamps.

Remarks. Feeds mostly on insects. Breeds in the park and is a common shrub nester. Often identified by its loud, cheery "sweet, sweet, sue-so-sweet" call. Builds a neat nest of plant fibers usually within the low branches of willows and alders.

BLACK-THROATED BLUE WARBLER (*Dendroica caerulescens*)

Description. Male has a black face, throat, and sides; female has white eyeline and square, white wing patch.
Distribution. Thick undergrowth.
Remarks. Tame and trusting; observer may be able to approach within a few feet.

BLACK-THROATED GREEN WARBLER (*Dendroica virens*)

Description. Throat and sides of breast are black; face is yellow; crown and upper parts are olive.
Distribution. Varies during migration.
Remarks. Common during migration. Has a distinctive song.

MAGNOLIA WARBLER (*Dendroica magnolia*)

Description. Male has bright yellow underparts with heavy black streaks. Black facial patch. Large white wing patch. Broad white patches on sides of tail. Female similar but dull. Four to five inches in length.
Distribution. Open stands of spruce and fir.
Remarks. Common migrant. Got its name from first specimen obtained by Alexander Wilson among magnolia trees in the early 1800s. Winters in Central America.

PALM WARBLER (*Dendroica palmarum*)

Description. Olive, drab, streaked, ground-feeding warbler with bright olive rump. Bright yellow undertail coverts. Reddish chestnut crown or cap during breeding season. Yellow eyebrow.
Distribution. Weedy fields and borders of marshes.
Remarks. Common migrant. One of the first to arrive in spring and last to depart in the fall.

WILSON'S WARBLER (*Wilsonia pusilla*)

Description. Male is olive green above and yellow below with black crown patch. Females have no markings.

Distribution. Moist thickets in woodlands and along streams.

Remarks. Uncommon migrant. Named for Scottish-American ornithologist-artist Alexander Wilson.

NORTHERN WATERTHRUSH (*Seiurus noveboracensis*)

Description. Sparrow-sized. Olive-brown upper parts; pale yellowish underparts with black streaks. Yellowish white line over eye, and streaked throat.

Distribution. Wooded swamps and lakeshores during breeding season. Wooded habitat during migration.

Remarks. Common migrant. Named for its resemblance to a thrush and its fondness of water.

AMERICAN REDSTART (*Setophaga ruticilla*)

Description. Male is black with bright orange patches on wings and tail; white belly. Female is dull: olive-brown above, white below with yellow wing and tail patches.

Distribution. Second-growth woodlands.

Remarks. Distinct habit of dropping down suddenly in pursuit of flying insects.

COMMON YELLOWTHROAT (*Geothlypis trichas*)

Description. Olive-brown above. Bright yellow throat and upper breast. Male has bold, black face mask bordered above with white.

Distribution. Moist thickets and grassy marshes.

Remarks. Breeds in the park and is a common shrub nester. Cheerful "witchity, witchity, witchity" song.

RED-WINGED BLACKBIRD (*Agelaius phoeniceus*)

Description. Adult male is all black except for red-and-white bands on shoulders. Female is brown with light eyebrows. Measures seven and one-half to nine and one-half inches.

Distribution. Freshwater marshes, moist thickets, and wet fields.

Red-winged blackbird

Remarks. Arrives as early as February. Its distinctive territorial call and dramatic display of its red epaulets enliven the marshes of the park during early spring. Breeds in the park.

STARLING (*Sturnus vulgaris*)

Description. Short-tailed, chunky, iridescent black bird. Long, pointed bill is yellow in summer and dark in winter. Pointed, triangular wings. Plumage speckled with whitish marks.

Distribution. Cities, suburbs, and farms. Flocks of starlings found throughout the park, especially in open grassy areas.

Remarks. Very common. Nonnative. Aggressive cavity nester that often displaces native cavity-nesting birds.

EASTERN MEADOWLARK (*Sturnella magna*)

Description. Stocky, brown-streaked bird with white-edged tail. Bright yellow throat and breast. Breast crossed by a black V.

Distribution. Meadows, pastures, and prairies.

Remarks. Occasionally overwinters at Floyd Bennett Field. Regular visitor to Gateway grasslands. Beautiful, melancholy song. Breeds in the park.

COMMON GRACKLE (*Quiscalus quiscula*)

Description. Long, wedge-shaped tail. Appears all black but is highly iridescent. Bright yellow eyes.

Distribution. Lawns, parks, fields, and open woodland.

Remarks. Loud, gregarious birds. Most common during early spring migrations.

BROWN-HEADED COWBIRD (*Molothrus ater*)

Description. Male is black with glossy brown head. Female is plain gray. Both have finchlike bills.

Distribution. Fields, woodland edges, and suburban areas.

Remarks. Parasite of yellow warbler nests especially. Lays eggs in other birds' nests.

BOBOLINK (*Dolichonyx oryzivorus*)

Description. Breeding male is largely black with a white rump and back. Dull yellow nape. Short, finchlike bill. Female is tan with brown streak over eyes.

Distribution. Moist, open fields and meadows.

Remarks. Uncommon migrant.

SNOW BUNTING (*Plectrophenax nivalis*)

Description. Sparrow-sized. Breeding male has black back with much white on head, underparts, wings, and tail.

Distribution. Arctic tundra. Large numbers observed on runways at Floyd Bennett Field.

Remarks. Small flocks usually winter at Breezy Point. As you approach the group, they flutter upward en masse and then light back on the ground, almost in unison.

Snow bunting

INDIGO BUNTING (*Passerina cyanea*)

Description. Sparrow-sized. Male is deep, brilliant blue with purplish head. Female is drab brown, paler beneath. Both have a short conical bill.

Distribution. Overgrown pastures, forest edges, and damp shrubs near water.

Remarks. Uncommon migrant. Beneficial to farmers because it consumes insect pests and weed seeds.

RUFOUS-SIDED TOWHEE (*Pipilo erythrophthalmus*)

Description. Female is warm brown and male is black. Male has black head and upper parts, white underparts, bright rufous patches on flanks.

Distribution. Thickets and bushy woodland edges.

Remarks. Common shrub- and ground-nesting species. Named towhee in 1731 by naturalist and bird artist Mark Catesby, in imitation of call note.

HOUSE FINCH (*Carpodacus mexicanus*)

Description. Male has red forehead, eyebrow, and throat. Brown-streaked belly and flesh. Female has an unpatterned head with distinct streaks on underside. Measures five to five and one-half inches.
Distribution. Cities and residential areas.
Remarks. Year-round resident. Common at bird feeders.

AMERICAN GOLDFINCH (*Carduelis tristis*)

Description. Breeding male is bright yellow with a white rump, black forehead, white edges on black wings and tail, and yellow at bend of wing. Female is duller and grayer with black rump, tail, and white wing bars.
Distribution. Bushy thickets, weedy grasslands, and trees.
Remarks. Common year-round. Likes feeders. Breeds in the park.

HOUSE SPARROW (*Passer domesticus*)

Description. Black bill. Black throat and eye patch. Gray crown. White wing bar. Measures five and one-half to six and one-quarter inches.
Distribution. Cities, towns, and agricultural areas.
Remarks. Becoming quite rare.

AMERICAN TREE SPARROW (*Spizella arborea*)

Description. Gray head with rufous crown and ear stripe. Upper parts are streaked with brown. Underparts are plain gray with dark spot in the center of the breast.
Distribution. Arctic willow and birch thickets, fields, weedy woodland edges, and roadside thickets in winter.
Remarks. Winter resident.

CHIPPING SPARROW (*Spizella passerina*)

Description. Small sparrow. Upper parts are brown, streaked with black. Underparts, sides of face, and rump are gray. Chestnut crown. White eyebrow with thin, black line through eye. Length is four and one-half to five and one-half inches.

Distribution. Grassy woodland edges, bushy pastures, and lawns.

Remarks. Breeds in the park and is an abundant migrant. Lines its nest with hair, and hence also called hairbird. Evergreens are its favorite nesting site.

FIELD SPARROW (*Spizella pusilla*)

Description. Bright pink bill. Rufous cap. White eye ring. Unstreaked buff breast. Five to six inches in length.

Distribution. Abandoned fields and pastures, scattered bushes, forest edges.

Remarks. Uncommon migrant. Breeds in the park.

VESPER SPARROW (*Pooecetes gramineus*)

Description. Grayish, streaked sparrow with white outer tail feathers. Narrow, white eye ring. Small patch of chestnut on band of wing.

Distribution. Fields and pastures.

Remarks. Rare migrant. Likes open fields.

SAVANNAH SPARROW (*Passerculus sandwichensis*)

Description. Pale and streaked, with a bright yellow eyebrow and flesh-colored legs. Notched tail.

Distribution. Fields, prairies, salt marshes, and grassy dunes. Seen at Breezy Point.

Remarks. Winter resident. The large, pale ipswich sparrow of winter sand dunes may be a race of this species.

SWAMP SPARROW (*Melospiza georgiana*)

Description. Chunky, dark sparrow with unstreaked underparts. Bright rufous cap. Rusty wings. Dark brown back and tail. Gray face and breast. White throat.

Distribution. Freshwater marshes and open, wooded swamps.

Remarks. Nests in low-lying areas. Breeds in the park.

White-throated sparrow

WHITE-THROATED SPARROW (*Zonotrichia albicollis*)

Description. Upper parts are streaked. Underparts are gray. Head has black and white stripes. Sharply defined throat patch. Dark bill. Yellow spot is visible between the eye and bill. Five and one-half to six and one-half inches long.

Distribution. Bushy undergrowth in coniferous woodland.

Remarks. Common winter resident.

DARK-EYED JUNCO (*Junco hyemalis*)

Description. Dark gray head, back, breast, and sides. Pink bill. Measures five to six and one-half inches.

Distribution. Coniferous or mixed forests. Winters in fields, gardens, parks, and thickets.

Remarks. Winter resident. Formerly called slate-colored junco.

BUTTERFLIES

Butterflies play an important role in the pollination of plants and are found in a variety of habitats, including open fields, thickets, and salt marshes.

This chapter includes species found on Ruler's Bar Hassock in the Jamaica Bay Wildlife Refuge and along perimeter areas of Jamaica Bay, including Floyd Bennett Field and Crooke's Point on the Staten Island unit. Depending on when you visit the park, you may be able to join a butterfly walk; call the Wildlife Refuge at (718) 318-4340. The best time of year to see butterflies is usually from March through early November or first frost.

The Family Papilionidae

All butterflies in this family have antennae whose tips are knobbed but not hooked. Their common name is derived from the long tail that projects from the hind wings. These butterflies are black, yellow, or white.

BLACK SWALLOWTAIL (*Papilio polyxenes*)

Description. Black with two rows of yellow spots around the wing edges.

Remarks. Often seen gathering nectar from milkweeds, thistles, and red clover. Has two broods annually. Larval food plants include Queen Anne's lace.

TIGER SWALLOWTAIL (*Papilio glaucus*)

Description. Yellow wings with black, tigerlike stripes.
Remarks. Only yellow swallowtail. Common along woodland edges

Black swallowtail

and gardens. Larval food plants include wild cherry, birch, and aspen. Peak time for observing these large, beautiful insects is July.

SPICEBUSH SWALLOWTAIL *(Papilio troilus)*

Description. Dark with whitish to yellowish spots along wing edges.

Remarks. Generally uncommon but can be seen in forested areas, such as the swamp white oak forest on Staten Island. May visit thistles in late summer. Larval food plants are sassafras and spicebush.

PIPEVINE SWALLOWTAIL *(Battus philenor)*

Description. Dark, with lower wing and top wing edge an iridescent blue-green.

Remarks. Uncommon in Northeast. First recorded in Jamaica Bay in 1986. Common along Palisades, New Jersey, where the larvae feeds on pipevine.

The Family Pieridae

The members of this family are white, yellow, or orange and have rounded wings. They use their full-sized forelegs for walking.

CHECKERED WHITE (*Pontia protodice*)

Description. White with brownish black spots.
Remarks. Irregular immigrant from the South to sandy coastal plains in the Northeast; arrives in late summer.

CABBAGE WHITE (*Pieris rapae*)

Description. Wings are yellowish white with black tip on forewings.
Remarks. Very common butterfly in open fields. The caterpillar feeds in plants of the cabbage family. Introduced species, considered a pest in the caterpillar stage.

CLOUDED SULPHUR (*Colias philodice*)

Description. Yellow with wide, black border containing yellow spots.
Remarks. Uncommon yellow butterfly of open fields.

ORANGE SULPHUR (*Colias eurytheme*)

Description. Large, orange with dark, wide bands.
Remarks. Most common sulphur. Found in open fields.

CLOUDLESS SULPHUR (*Phoebis sennae*)

Description. Unmarked color varies from yellow to orange to green.
Remarks. Largest yellow butterfly. Usually seen in Northeast during late summer.

LITTLE YELLOW (*Eurema lisa*)

Description. Pale, often white with dark border.
Remarks. Rare species. Small colony persists at Marine Park, on the north shore of Jamaica Bay.

VARIEGATED FRITILLARY (*Euptoieta claudia*)

Description. Dull orange-brown, dark brown markings, and paler shades.
Remarks. Late summer migrant. Absent some years.

GREAT SPANGLED FRITILLARY (*Speyeria cybele*)

Description. Wings above are orange-brown with many black spots. Forewings below are paler with brownish black markings and a few silvery yellow spots. Hind wings are darker with silvery spots edged in black.
Remarks. Rare at Gateway. Common just north of New York City.

PEARL CRESCENT (*Phyciodes tharos*)

Description. Wings are mostly brownish orange marked with dark brown. Wings below are brighter orange with fewer marks.
Remarks. Common in wet meadows.

QUESTION MARK (*Polygonia interrogationis*)

Description. Wings above are tawny, brownish orange with black spots and pale lilac around margin. Darker hind wings. Wings below have silvery marking resembling a question mark.
Remarks. Cryptic coloration and secretive habits make it hard to find.

COMMA (*Polygonia comma*)

Description. Brown beneath with smooth wing margins. No silver coloring. Similar to the Question Mark.
Remarks. Uncommon to rare at Gateway.

MOURNING CLOAK (*Nymphalis antiopa*)

Description. Wings above are black with blue spots and whitish edge.

Remarks. Overwinters as adult. First butterfly of spring, appearing in early March.

AMERICAN LADY (*Vanessa virginiensis*)

Description. Brownish, with blue spots along edge of lower wing.

Remarks. Commonly seen feeding on wildflowers.

PAINTED LADY (*Vanessa cardui*)

Description. Brownish with five black spots along edge of lower wing.

Remarks. Common some years; absent others.

COMPTON'S TORTOISE SHELL (*Nymphalis vau-album*)

Description. Large with white spots on upper edge of upper and lower wing.

Remarks. Very rare. Only two records at Gateway.

RED ADMIRAL (*Vanessa atalanta*)

Description. Brown with orange band along edge of lower wing and also orange band from lower edge across wing at an angle.

Remarks. Common.

BUCKEYE (*Junonia coenia*)

Description. Wings are mostly olive-brown with whitish yellow mark at tip, with one spot toward bottom of front wing. Hind wings have two spots, one larger than the other.

Remarks. Common in late summer. Absent some years. Common southern species.

RED-SPOTTED PURPLE (*Limenitis arthemis astyanax*)

Description. Greenish blue with red spots along margin.
Remarks. Rare to uncommon most years. More common in the South.

VICEROY (*Limenitis archippus*)

Description. Mimics the monarch butterfly. Wings are brownish orange with dark edges and veins. Forewings have two white spots near the tip along the front margin and white dots in a black band along the edge.
Remarks. Rare.

TAWNY EMPEROR (*Asterocampa clyton*)

Description. Large eyespots on hind wings and black streak beyond middle of forewings.
Remarks. Hackberry feeders. Common at Sandy Hook.

The Family Satyridae

These butterflies are dull brown or tawny with at least one eyespot on each wing.

LITTLE WOOD SATYR (*Megisto cymela*)

Description. Light brown with two eyespots on each wing. Lower wing has smaller eyespots along wing edge.
Remarks. Uncommon.

WOOD NYMPH (*Cercyonis pegala*)

Description. Dark brown wings. Each forewing has yellow patch containing two blue eyespots edged with black.

The Family Danaidae

This family contains butterflies that are toxic to predators. They feed on milkweed and other poisonous plants.

MONARCH (*Danaus plexippus*)

Description. Orange-brown wings; dark margins with two rows of orange or white spots, sometimes both, three to four inches long. Resembles the viceroy.

Remarks. Common along beaches in late summer. Migrates to Mexico. Feeds on the nectar of milkweed plant ingesting substances that make it toxic to birds and other predators.

The Family Hesperiidae

These insects have some characteristics of both moths and butterflies. Skippers are distinguished from true butterflies by their antennae, which are farther apart at the base and end in pointed, curved clubs. They are named for their skipping flight patterns.

SILVER-SPOTTED SKIPPER (*Epargyreus clarus*)

Description. Brown wings. Forewings have a golden band below. Hind wings have white fringe with larger, silvery white, irregular spot.

Remarks. Common large skipper. Feeds on locusts.

JUVENAL'S DUSKYWING (*Erynnis juvenalis*)

Description. Large and brown with eight large, white spots on upper wing and two smaller white spots on lower wing.

Remarks. Uncommon.

HORACE'S DUSKYWING (*Erynnis horatius*)

Description. Similar to juvenal's duskywing but has six white spots on forewing.

Remarks. Uncommon.

COMMON SOOTYWING (*Pholisora catullus*)

Description. Dark wings with two curved rows of small, white spots on each forewing. Dark underwing.

Remarks. Likes open, disturbed habitats.

CHECKERED SKIPPER (*Pyrgus communis*)

Description. Male has pale gray wings. Female has black wings. Both have many white spots, which give them a checkered appearance. Has blue hairs on body and wing bases.

Remarks. Rare late-summer migrant. Found on mallow (*Malva*) at Floyd Bennett Field greenhouse.

The Subfamily Hesperiinae

The adults in this subfamily are usually yellow to orange-brown with dark markings and borders. They are important pollinators.

LEAST SKIPPER (*Ancyloxypha numitor*)

Description. Black forewing with orange center; underside is black and orange. Hind wings are orange with black border; underside is orange. Antennae ends in blunt club.

Remarks. Likes wet, grassy areas.

PECK'S SKIPPER (*Polites coras*)

Description. Small with distinct yellow patches on underside.
Remarks. Common. Likes disturbed habitats.

SWARTHY SKIPPER (*Nastra l'herminier*)

Description. Neutral colors, dull, drab.
Remarks. Small, nondescript skipper. Common in late summer.

NORTHERN BROKEN DASH (*Wallengrenia egeremet*)

Description. Brown wings with a few small, yellow spots. Male has black band broken by a patch of shiny scales, hence its name. Underside of hind wings is purple-brown with faint crescent of paler spots.

Remarks. Common skipper in summer.

ZABULON SKIPPER *(Poanes zabulon)*

Description. Yellow underwings with row of dark spots from wing center to body.

Remarks. Likes trailsides; feeds on grasses. Sexually dimorphic.

BROAD-WINGED SKIPPER *(Poanes viator)*

Description. Large and broad-winged; extensive dark areas on top.

Remarks. Common in July and August near marshes. Larva feeds on *Phragmites*.

SALT-MARSH SKIPPER *(Panoquina panoquin)*

Description. Distinctive white, longitudinal dash on lower wing.

Remarks. Uncommon. Found on flowers near marshes. Larva feeds on *Distichlis* (spike grass).

MAMMALS

The black bear, red fox, bison, puma, wolf, and otter are all native to New York City. Unless you're at the Bronx Zoo, however, you will never see them here again. All are locally extinct because of loss of their habitats. This is not to say that there are no mammals at Gateway. The park is home to scores of them: field mice, shrews, opossums, rabbits, raccoons, chipmunks, squirrels, meadow voles, muskrats, and three species of bats all provide food for harriers and consume plenty of insects.

Marsupials

OPOSSUM *(Didelphis virginiana)*

Description. Nocturnal marsupial, or pouched mammal. White face, black ear, hairless tail, pointed nose, heavy body, and short legs. Measures twenty-four to forty inches and weighs nine to thirteen pounds.

Distribution. Woodlands and along streams. Common at Sandy Hook in Maritime Forest and seen occasionally on Staten Island and in the Jamaica Bay unit.

Remarks. Female and young observed in hollowed-out old holly tree trunks along the Sandy Hook trails. North America's only marsupial. They have fifty teeth, more than any other North American land mammal.

Shrews

SHORT-TAILED SHREW *(Blarina brevicanda)*

Description. Three to four inches in length (head and body); tail three-quarters to one inch long. Dark metallic gray.

Distribution. Very abundant; well distributed in eastern United States.

Remarks. Litters up to eight young; has two breeding seasons. Unique among North American mammals in that it has venomous saliva, which probably aids in subduing its prey. Eats insects.

Bats

LITTLE BROWN MYOTIS (*Myotis lucifugus*)

Description. Small bat. Gets its sheen from hairs on its back that have long, glossy tips. Medium-size ears. One-and-one-half-inch forearms.

Hoary bat

Distribution. Individuals seen at Gateway are migrants. Found park-wide nesting in hollow trees and buildings. Abundant in North America.

Remarks. In spring and fall, seen at dusk flying over grasslands. Often mistaken for birds; they can be differentiated from birds, however, by careful observation of their extreme zigzagging flight. Feeds on insects, using echolocation to find prey.

RED BAT (*Lasiurus borealis*)

Description. Males are brick red to rusty red with white-tipped hairs. Females are lighter in color. Tail membrane is fully furred on top. Forearms are one and one-half to one and two-thirds inches long.

Distribution. Uncommon migrant found in wooded areas.

Remarks. Passes through Gateway area during its southward migration.

HOARY BAT (*Lasiurus cinereus*)

Description. Hair has white tips. Buffy throat. Rounded ears. Furry tail membrane. Forearm extends over two inches.

Distribution. Infrequently recorded migrant found in wooded areas.

Remarks. Very rare: only three sightings of this bat at Gateway, the last in 1986.

Rabbits

EASTERN COTTONTAIL (*Sylvilagus floridanus*)

Description. Brownish or grayish body. Whitish feet. Nape patch is reddish. White cottony tail. Measures fourteen to seventeen inches.

Distribution. Found in field, shrub, and woodland edge habitats throughout Gateway.

Remarks. Varied diet. Its ability to avoid predation and its adaptability to new habitats have enabled this species to colonize.

BLACK-TAILED JACKRABBIT (*Lepus californicus*)

Description. Black on top of tail and rump. Black-tipped ears. Measures seventeen to twenty-one inches.

Distribution. Found only on JoCo Marsh in Jamaica Bay, adjacent to John F. Kennedy International Airport.

Remarks. This western species was accidentally introduced in the 1950s when some jackrabbits escaped from a crate at the airport.

Squirrels

EASTERN CHIPMUNK (*Tamias striatus*)

Description. Small with facial stripes. Has body stripes that end at rump. Bushy tail. Measures up to six inches, with a tail three to four and a half inches long.

Distribution. Limited to the main island of Jamaica Bay Wildlife Refuge and its gardens.

Remarks. Introduced in 1985. A small population has been established at the refuge. They are basically ground-dwelling squirrels. Their extensive burrows are up to twelve feet long and may include a storage chamber, sleeping room, dump, and latrine.

GRAY SQUIRREL (*Sciurus carolinensis*)

Description. Grayish. Very bushy tail bordered with white-tipped hairs. Measures eight to ten inches.

Distribution. Found throughout Gateway. Nests in trees and buildings.

Remarks. Gray squirrels at Gateway are very adaptable. Because large trees and acorns are scarce, many gray squirrels make nests of leaves and feed on pine cones and bayberries.

Mice

WHITE-FOOTED MOUSE (*Peromyscus leucopus*)

Description. White belly and feet. Upper parts are pale to rich reddish brown. Tail is usually shorter than head and body. Measures three and three-fifths to four and one-fifth inches.

Distribution. Widespread. Found in most woodland and shrubby habitats at Gateway.

Remarks. This mammal feeds on bayberry and black cherry.

HOUSE MOUSE (*Mus musculus*)

Description. Grayish brown with gray or buffy belly. Scaly tail. Measures three and one-fifth to three and two-fifths inches.

Distribution. Found throughout Gateway in grasslands, shrub, and wooded areas.

Remarks. Feeds on grasses, bark, nuts, and berries. Preyed on by smaller hawks and owls.

Other Rodents

MEADOW VOLE (*Microtus pennsylvanicus*)

Description. Belly is silvery to slightly buffy or dark gray, and tail is bicolored. Fur is long and soft. Measures three and a half to five inches, with a tail one and one-half to two and one-half inches long.

Distribution. Most common mammal at Gateway. Found in fields, grasslands, and salt marshes throughout the park.

Remarks. Major prey of many hawks, owls, and snakes. Prolific reproduction. A female can have more than one hundred young annually.

MUSKRAT (*Ondatra zibethicus*)

Description. Dense, rich, brown fur. Long, naked, ratlike tail that is flattened on sides. Measures ten to fourteen inches.

Distribution. Found in freshwater and saltwater marshes and at edges of ponds throughout Gateway.

Remarks. Feeds on shoots of aquatic plants. Lives in both bank dens and "houses" made of vegetation.

NORWAY RAT (*Rattus norvegicus*)

Description. Grayish brown with a grayish belly. Long, scaly tail. Measures seven to ten inches.

Distribution. Exotic Asian species introduced to North America by Europeans. Now common throughout Gateway. Burrows near bayberry. Clumps can be detected by excavated sand.

Remarks. These rats are omnivorous. A major food source for barn owls and hawks, they have up to five litters per year with eight to ten young per litter.

Raccoons

RACCOON (*Procyon lotor*)

Description. Medium-sized with black mask and whitish and black rings on tail. Measures eighteen to twenty-eight inches.

Distribution. Commonly seen at Sandy Hook, and is becoming increasingly common throughout the Staten Island and Jamaica Bay units.

Remarks. Omnivore that may carry rabies. It can be a major predator of turtle eggs, particularly if population is increased through food provided by humans.

THE FUTURE OF GATEWAY

Gateway inherited a considerable number of abandoned but historically important buildings. Their upkeep, along with infrastructure repair, has somewhat impeded the park's ability to concentrate on preserving and protecting its natural and recreational features. Since the completion of the park's general management plan in 1979, the purpose of this bistate national park unit has been extended beyond beach use and wildlife observation. This direction, however, still is muddied by the lack of appropriate funding and staffing levels necessary to foster long-term environmental education, as well as a diversity of public programs. Short-term recreational uses such as team sports and festivals do not satisfy the needs of an urban populace seeking to escape from the everyday city life. To observe a monarch butterfly gathering the nectar from goldenrod on its migration south, to glimpse an osprey fishing in the coastal lagoons of Sandy Hook, to see toads in a pond at an abandoned airfield, or at sunset to see a barn owl returning to its nest with food for its young—all these images might be, for a million schoolchildren and for fourteen million metropolitan area residents, their only connection to living things and to the beautiful complexity and intricacy that is urban biological diversity.

I didn't have to go as far as Alaska to see a snowy owl. I went instead to Fort Tilden and Floyd Bennett Field, both in Brooklyn, New York, not far from my home. Seeing my first snowy there may have been more incredible—it certainly was more relevant—than reading a description of one gliding over the tundra landscape of Alaska.

I believe that as long as we approach urban national parks as part of our fabric of life, the natural system will survive and regenerate to earlier forms of productivity. We should remember that Gateway's foundation is its natural and cultural resources, which the United States Congress has declared as having national significance. We must make every effort to preserve such resources so that future generations can enjoy Gateway and other urban national parks. As Joseph L. Sax stated in *Mountains without Handrails: Reflections on the National Parks*, "The growth of the national park system is justified by a recognition that the symbolism of parks needs to be brought closer to the public, not that the symbol should be urbanized." Gateway will provide this symbolism into the future.

◆

INTERESTING NEARBY SITES

New York Zoological Society, the Wildlife Conservation Society *(includes the Bronx Zoological Park and the Aquarium for Wildlife Conservation)*

In addition to the Bronx Zoo, the NYZS maintains zoos in Queens, Central Park in Manhattan, and Prospect Park in Brooklyn. These three latest additions were once part of the city zoo system but have recently been taken over by the society. The aquarium at Coney Island is also a part of this world-renowned conservation society. The aquarium and Gateway conduct cooperative research in the Park.

New York City Parks and Recreation

Included under its management are Central Park in Manhattan and Prospect Park in Brooklyn. There are also more than 26,000 acres of open space, including Kissena, Van Courtland, Flushing Meadows, and Marine Park, that are part of the New York City Parks' system. Ninety-five percent of the open spaces in the five boroughs of New York City belong to the City and National Park units.

American Museum of Natural History

The American Museum of Natural History is widely acknowledged to have the greatest collection of fossil vertebrates in the world, and its dinosaur and other fossil halls, which were recently renovated, draw on more than a century of research by the museum's scientists to tell the story of the evolution of life. Two halls devoted to fossil mammals opened in 1994, with highlights ranging from saber-toothed cats, mammoths, and mastodons to some of our earliest relatives—bizarre, reptilelike crea-

142

tures with three-foot sails along their backs. Opened in spring 1995, the new dinosaur halls feature dozens of dinosaurs grouped according to their evolutionary relationships and reflect new scientific insights into the history of life on earth. The museum will soon include an exhibit on primitive vertebrates.

The hall of human biology and evolution, the museum's newest permanent hall, examines the heritage we share with other living things, traces the complex pattern of human evolution, and explores the qualities that make us unique. The hall uses the latest multimedia technology and sophisticated exhibit techniques to explore these issues. In addition, the new hall is the only major exhibition in the country to investigate in depth the mysteries of human evolution, featuring four life-size dioramas depicting scenes of our early relatives. The museum and Gateway cooperate on mutually important biodiversity and conservation research and issues.

Great Swamp National Wildlife Refuge

Established in 1960, the refuge lies twenty-six miles west of New York City's Times Square and seven miles south of Morristown, New Jersey. Swamp woodland, hardwood ridges, cattail marsh, and grassland typify this approximately 7,000-acre refuge. The swamp contains many large old oak and beech trees, stands of mountain laurel, and plants of both northern and southern botanical zones. The refuge bird leaflet lists more than 222 species of birds according to their seasonal occurrence. (The Raptor Trust, Inc., a rehabilitation center where visitors can get a closer look at hawks, owls, and other birds of prey, is located within the refuge in Bernardsville, New Jersey.) Mammals found in the refuge include the white-tailed deer, river otter, muskrat, raccoon, skunk, red fox, woodchuck, gray squirrel, opossum, and cottontail rabbit. Fish, reptiles, and amphibians, including the state's endangered bog turtle and blue-spotted salamander, are also found in the refuge. Visitors are encouraged to observe, study, photograph, and just walk through this natural environment. The best times for observing wildlife are early morning and late afternoon.

Fire Island National Seashore

This includes the smallest designated wilderness area in the U.S. National Park System. In 1980 the seven-mile (eleven-kilometer) stretch of Fire

Island from Smith Point West to Watch Hill, an area of approximately 1,400 acres (570 hectares), was designated by Congress as wilderness, the only area in New York State to be set aside in this manner. With the exception of the boardwalk trail for the handicapped at Smith Point West, the wilderness is accessible only by foot. If you're willing to invest the time and energy necessary to hike it, the wilderness will reward you with a view of the island as it must have been when the first Europeans saw it 400 years ago. Every swale and every grove of pines has its own fascination. No matter what the season, fishing is good. In Great South Bay, you will find bluefish, striped bass, winter flounder, and other species. In the surf you can cast for striped bass, bluefish, mackerel, and weakfish. Not to be missed is the Sunken Forest, so called because of its location down behind the dunes, directly west of Sailors Haven. Gnarled holly, sassafras, tupelo, and shadblow form the canopy, and vines of catbrier, poison ivy, and wild grape climb from the forest floor toward the sun.

Buffer the Bay Program

Many people would envision a national park to be an area that is removed from a city's congestion and chaos. But unlike most national parks, Gateway National Recreation Area is located minutes from expressways, parkways, international airports, and bus lines. Housing and industries have expanded and threaten to take over adjacent open space valuable as scenic corridors and needed by migrating birds and insects. For Jamaica Bay to maintain its function as a preserve, it has become necessary to establish buffers between the bay and the city surrounding it. The Buffer the Bay project recommends improvements and enhancements of Jamaica Bay by preventing further degradation from development. With this protection the bay will be allowed to maintain its roles as a migratory stopover, a roosting site, a natural filter for runoff, and a public viewing area.

The Trust for Public Land, in cooperation with the New York City Chapter of the Audubon Society, surveyed properties adjacent to the park in need of protection. The southeastern group consists of Mott Point, Edgemere Landfill, Somerville Basin, Dubose Point, Brant Point, Norton Basin, and Vernam Basin. Northern Jamaica Bay includes Spring Creek, Fresh Creek Basin, Paerdegat Basin, and Four Sparrow Marsh. These two major areas are separated by John F. Kennedy International Airport. Ask the Trust for Public Lands for a copy of the survey report.

For More Information

When you visit the park, ask about groups that both protect and enjoy the natural resources that are Gateway National Recreation Area.

Since Gateway's beginnings, the members of the Sierra Club's and the Audubon Society's New York City chapters have been at the forefront of environmental awareness and planning for the park. Through effective congressional lobbying and education, they have assisted in shaping the General Management Plan for Gateway. Sierra Club and Audubon Society volunteers have participated in most of the park's natural resource programs—from plover protection activities to lecture series.

Other groups of note include the Linnean Society, Friends of Gateway, the Brooklyn Butterfly Club, Educators for Gateway, and the Gateway Environmental Study Center.

Over the more than twenty years of the park's existence, many academic institutions have used the park as a laboratory, providing research and information critical to the park's resource protection: Polytechnic University, Brooklyn College, Queens College, Yale University, Richmond College, Columbia University, St. John's University, Brookdale Community College, Rutgers University, Harvard University, SUNY Stony Brook, and Kingsborough Community College.

BIRD LIST

Because the park is along the Atlantic flyway, you have a good chance at seeing most of the birds on this list. The abundance and distribution of species varies considerably both seasonally and throughout the habitats of the Hudson-Raritan ecosystem. Be sure to note your observations in the logbooks kept by park rangers at the visitor centers throughout the park. At the trail head of the West Pond in Jamaica Bay Wildlife Refuge is a logbook containing a record of bird sightings for the past twenty years.

This list is not a rigorous ornithological listing; it is just a means for visitors to record birds observed in the park.

Status Symbols

C *Abundant:* more than 30 individuals are usually recorded every visit; and *Common:* 10 to 30 individuals usually recorded every visit.

U *Uncommon:* 1 to 9 individuals per visit, sometimes missed.

R *Rare:* only one or a few individuals recorded throughout the season, often missed.

V *Very rare:* recorded sporadically, not seen every year.

Ducks, Geese, and Swans
  Swan
____ Tundra (R)
____ Mute (C)
____ Snow Goose (U)
____ Brant (C)
____ Canada Goose (C)
____ Wood Duck (R)
____ Green-winged Teal (C)

____ Black Duck (C)
____ Mallard (C)
____ Pintail (C)
____ Blue-winged Teal (C)
____ Northern Shoveler (C)
____ Gadwall (C)
  Wigeon
____ Eurasian (R)
____ American (C)

____ Canvasback (C)
____ Redhead (U)
____ Ring-necked Duck (R)
Scaup
____ Greater (C)
____ Lesser (C)
____ Common Goldeneye (C)
____ Bufflehead (C)
Merganser
____ Hooded (U)
____ Red-breasted (C)
____ Ruddy Duck (C)

Shorebirds
Plover
____ Black-bellied (C)
____ American Golden (R)
____ Semipalmated (C)
____ Piping (U)
____ Killdeer (C)
____ American Oystercatcher (C)
____ American Avocet (V)
Yellowlegs
____ Greater (C)
____ Lesser (C)
Cormorant
____ Great (U)
____ Double-crested (C)
Bittern
____ American (U)
____ Least (U)
Herons and Egrets
____ Great Blue (C)
____ Great Egret (C)
____ Snowy Egret (C)
____ Little Blue (U)
____ Tricolored Heron (U)

____ Cattle Egret (U)
____ Green (C)
Night Heron
____ Black-crowned (C)
____ Yellow-crowned (U)
____ Glossy Ibis (C)
____ Willet (C)
____ Spotted Sandpiper (C)
____ Upland Sandpiper (V)
____ Whimbrel (R)
Godwit
____ Hudsonian (R)
____ Marbled (R)
____ Ruddy Turnstone (C)
____ Red Knot (C)
____ Sanderling (C)
Sandpiper
____ Semipalmated (C)
____ Western (U)
____ Least (C)
____ White-rumped (U)
____ Baird's (R)
____ Pectoral (U)
____ Dunlin (C)
____ Curlew (R)
____ Stilt (R)
Dowitcher
____ Short-billed (C)
____ Long-billed (R)
____ Common Snipe (C)
____ American Woodcock (U)
Phalarope
____ Wilson's (U)

Hawks, Eagles, and Falcons
____ Osprey (U)
____ Bald Eagle (V)

____ Northern Harrier (C)
Hawk
____ Sharp-shinned (U)
____ Cooper's (U)
____ Goshawk (R)
____ Red-shouldered (V)
____ Broad-winged (V)
____ Red-tailed (R)
____ Rough-legged (R)
____ American Kestrel (C)
____ Merlin (U)
____ Peregrine Falcon (U)

Pheasants and Quails
____ Ring-necked Pheasant (C)
____ Northern Bobwhite (C)

Rails
____ Clapper Rail (U)
____ Virginia (U)
____ Sora (U)
____ Common Moorhen (U)
____ American Coot (C)

Gulls, Terns, and Skimmers
Gulls
____ Laughing (C)
____ Bonaparte's (U)
____ Ring-billed (C)
____ Herring (C)
____ Iceland (V)
____ Glaucous (V)
____ Great Black-backed (C)
Terns
____ Royal (V)
____ Roseate (R)
____ Common (C)

____ Forster's (C)
____ Least (C)
____ Black Skimmer (C)

Doves
____ Rock (C)
____ Mourning (C)

Owls
____ Barn (C)
____ Snowy (R)
____ Long-eared (R)
____ Short-eared (R)
____ Saw-whet (R)

Woodpeckers
____ Red-headed (R)
____ Red-bellied (R)
____ Yellow-bellied Sapsucker (U)
____ Downy (C)

Flycatchers
____ Olive-sided (V)
____ Yellow-bellied (R)
____ Acadian (V)
____ Alder (V)
____ Willow (U)
____ Least (R)
____ Eastern Phoebe (C)
____ Great Crested (R)
Kingbird
____ Western (V)
____ Eastern (U)

Swallows
____ Tree (C)
____ Rough-winged (C)
____ Bank (C)

____ Cliff (R)
____ Barn (C)

Crows
____ Blue Jay (U)
____ American (C)
____ Fish (C)

Nuthatches
____ Red-breasted (U)
____ White-breasted (R)

Wrens
____ Carolina (R)
____ House (U)
____ Winter (U)
____ Sedge (V)
____ Marsh (U)

Thrushes
____ Gray-cheeked (R)
____ Swainson's (U)
____ Hermit (U)
____ Wood (U)
____ American Robin (C)

Mimids
____ Gray Catbird (C)
____ Northern Mockingbird (C)
____ Brown Thrasher (U)
____ American Pipit (R)
____ Cedar Waxwing (U)
____ Starling (C)

Vireos
____ White-eyed (U)
____ Solitary (U)
____ Yellow-throated (R)

____ Warbling (R)
____ Philadelphia (R)
____ Red-eyed (C)

Warblers
____ Blue-winged (R)
____ Golden-winged (R)
____ Tennessee (R)
____ Orange-crowned (R)
____ Nashville (U)
____ Parula (C)
____ Yellow (C)
____ Chestnut-sided (U)
____ Magnolia (C)
____ Cape May (C)
____ Black-throated Blue (C)
____ Yellow-rumped (C)
____ Black-throated Green (C)
____ Blackburnian (C)
____ Yellow-throated (V)
____ Pine (R)
____ Prairie (C)
____ Palm (C)
____ Bay-breasted (C)
____ Blackpoll (U)
____ Cerulean (R)
____ Black-and-white (C)
____ American Redstart (C)
____ Prothonotary (V)
____ Worm-eating (R)
____ Common Yellowthroat (C)

Sparrows
____ Tree (U)
____ Chipping (C)
____ Clay-colored (V)
____ Field (U)
____ Vesper (R)

____ Lark (R)
____ Savannah (C)
____ Grasshopper (U)
____ Sharp-tailed (C)
____ Seaside (C)
____ Song Sparrow (C)
____ House Sparrow (C)

Finches and Blackbirds
____ Dark-eyed Junco (C)
____ Snow Bunting (U)
____ Bobolink (C)
____ Red-winged Blackbird (C)
____ Eastern Meadowlark (C)
Grackle
    ____ Boat-tailed (U)
    ____ Common (C)
____ Brown-headed Cowbird (C)
____ Northern Oriole (C)
____ Northern Cardinal (C)
Grosbeak
    ____ Rose-breasted (C)
    ____ Blue (R)

____ Indigo Bunting (U)
____ Dickcissel (R)
____ Rufous-sided Towhee (C)
____ Purple Finch (U)
____ House Finch (C)
Crossbill
    ____ Red (R)
    ____ White-winged (R)
____ Common Redpoll (R)
____ Pine Siskin (U)
____ American Goldfinch (C)
____ Evening Grosbeak (R)

Others
____ Common Nighthawk (R)
____ Whip-poor-will (R)
____ Chimney Swift (C)
____ Ruby-throated Hummingbird (R)
____ Belted Kingfisher (R)

FIELD GUIDE TO PLANTS AND ANIMALS

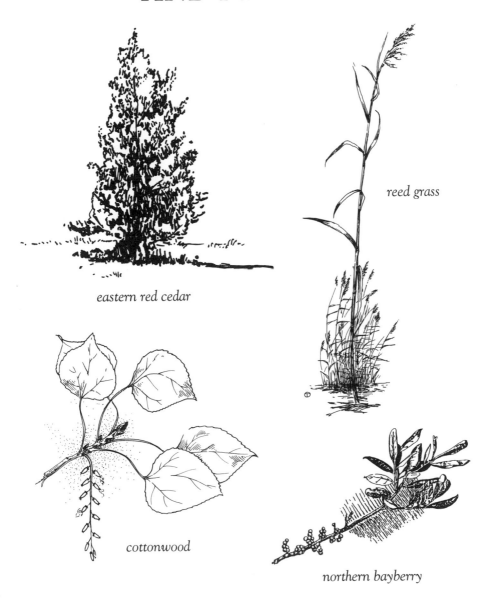

eastern red cedar

reed grass

cottonwood

northern bayberry

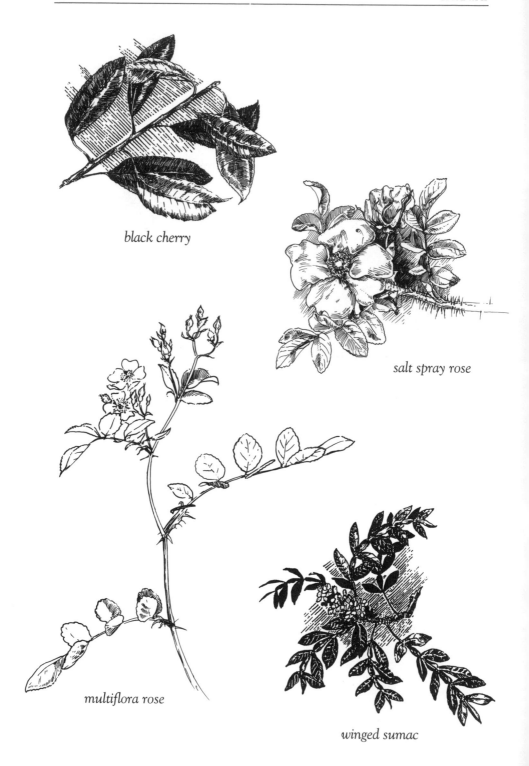

black cherry

salt spray rose

multiflora rose

winged sumac

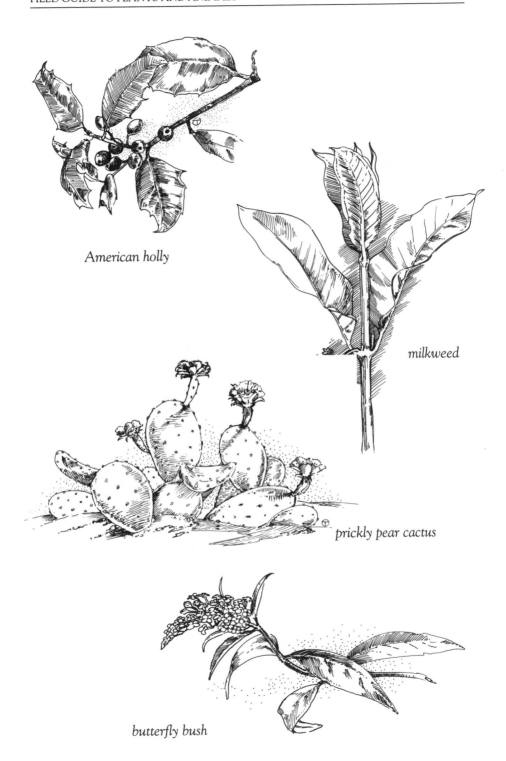

American holly

milkweed

prickly pear cactus

butterfly bush

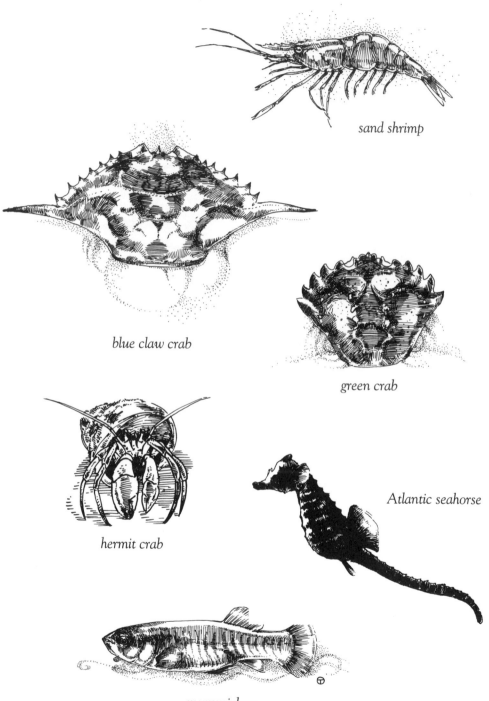

sand shrimp

blue claw crab

green crab

hermit crab

Atlantic seahorse

mummichog

bluefish

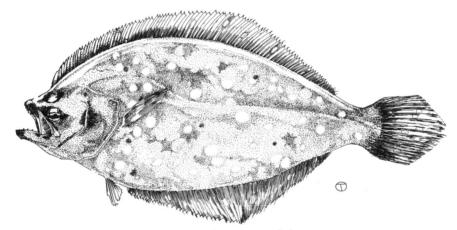

summer flounder or fluke

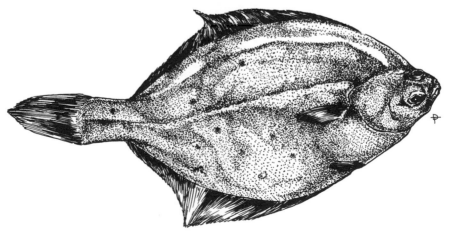

winter flounder

common garter snake

redback salamander

spring peeper

Fowler's toad and box turtle

Canada goose

double-crested cormorant

snowy egret

great egret

gadwall

black duck

semipalmated plover

greater yellowlegs

American oystercatcher

common tern

herring gull

great black-backed gull

American kestrel

ring-necked pheasant

downy woodpecker

house finch

saw-whet owl

cabbage white

orange sulphur

monarch

eastern cottontail

meadow vole

raccoon

Index

(Illustrations are indicated by page numbers in italics.)